TIME
21 DAYS
TO BAGHDAD

TIME
21 DAYS
TO BAGHDAD

**The Inside
Story of How
America Won
The War
Against Iraq**

CONTENTS

Previous Pages: A soldier with the Army's 3rd Infantry Division double-checks coordinates on the road to Baghdad, just outside the capital's airport
Photograph by Christopher Morris—VII

21 DAYS
TO BAGHDAD

"A prelude to the apocalypse"
a photojournalist called the
sandstorm that bathed Baghdad
and a statue of Saddam Hussein
in eerie light as U.S. forces bore
down on the city

**Photograph by
James Nachtwey—VII**

21 DAYS TO BAGHDAD

Editors	Steve Koepp
	Bill Saporito
Picture Editor	MaryAnne Golon
Art Director	Marti Golon
Editors at Large	Michael Elliott
	Nancy Gibbs
Chief of Reporters	Ellin Martens
Graphics Editor	Jackson Dykman
Deputy Art Director	Gigi Fava
Assistant Art Director	Avi Litwack
Deputy Picture Editors	Alice Gabriner
	Hillary Raskin
Assistant Picture Editor	Bill Carwin
Production Supervisor	Brian Fellows
Correspondents	Brian Bennett
	Sally B. Donnelly
	Meenakshi Ganguly
	Aparisim Ghosh
	Joshua Kucera
	Jim Lacey
	Terry McCarthy
	Alex Perry
	Andrew Purvis
	Paul Quinn-Judge
	Simon Robinson
	Michael Ware
	Michael Weisskopf
Photographers	Kate Brooks
	Thomas Dworzak
	James Hill, Yunghi Kim
	Yuri Kozyrev
	Benjamin Lowy
	Christopher Morris
	James Nachtwey
	Robert Nickelsberg
	Patrick Robert
Reporters	Kathleen Adams
	Nadia Mustafa
	Andrea Sachs

TIME Books

Time Inc. Home Entertainment

President Rob Gursha
Vice President, Branded Businesses David Arfine
Vice President, New Product Development
Richard Fraiman
Executive Director, Marketing Services Carol Pittard
Director, Retail & Special Sales Tom Mifsud
Director of Finance Tricia Griffin
Assistant Marketing Director Ann Marie Doherty
Prepress Manager Emily Rabin
Book Production Manager Jonathan Polsky
Associate Product Manager Sara Stumpf

Special Thanks: Bozena Bannett, Robert Dente,
Gina Di Meglio, Anne-Michelle Gallero, Peter Harper,
Suzanne Janso, Robert Marasco, Natalie McCrea,
Mary Jane Rigoroso, Steven Sandonato

Copyright 2003
Time Inc. Home Entertainment

Published by Time Books
Time Inc., 1271 Avenue of the Americas
New York, New York 10020

ISBN: 1-932273-12-3
Library of Congress Control Number: 2003106598

Time Books is a trademark of Time Inc.

We welcome your comments and suggestions about Time
Books. Please write to us at: Time Books (Attention: Book
Editors), P.O. Box 11016, Des Moines, Iowa 50336-1016
If you would like to order any of our hardcover Collector's
Edition books, please call us at 1-800-327-6388 (Monday
through Friday, 7:00 a.m.–8:00 p.m., or Saturday, 7:00
a.m.–6:00 p.m. Central Time).

In a column of vehicles on the outskirts of Baghdad, a Marine driver waits while a fire fight rages ahead

FOREWORD

FOUR HUNDRED-FOURTEEN DAYS PASSED FROM THE TIME PRESident Bush first named Iraq as part of an "axis of evil" to the time the first missiles flew. But after Gulf War II was launched, the campaign to topple Saddam Hussein's regime was one of the shortest, most intense military operations in history. U.S. and British soldiers and marines took just 21 days to sweep the 350 miles from the Kuwaiti border to downtown Baghdad. TIME covered the conflict in gripping detail, having dispatched a team of 10 photographers and 13 correspondents. Many of TIME's journalists

were embedded with the troops and experienced the campaign from their point of view—traveling with them, eating the same MREs and going into battle with them. Other TIME journalists roamed Iraq independently, from the mountains in the north to downtown Baghdad. You can't get any closer to war. In *21 Days to Baghdad*, TIME brings you the most extraordinary of those images and battlefield dispatches, in all their glory and sorrow.

The Editors of TIME

7

The Commander in Chief Pays a Call

President Bush addressed sailors and their families at Mayport Naval Station near Jacksonville, Fla., in February 2003. The lack of land bases made the use of carrier battle groups critical in the war

Photograph by Christopher Morris—VII

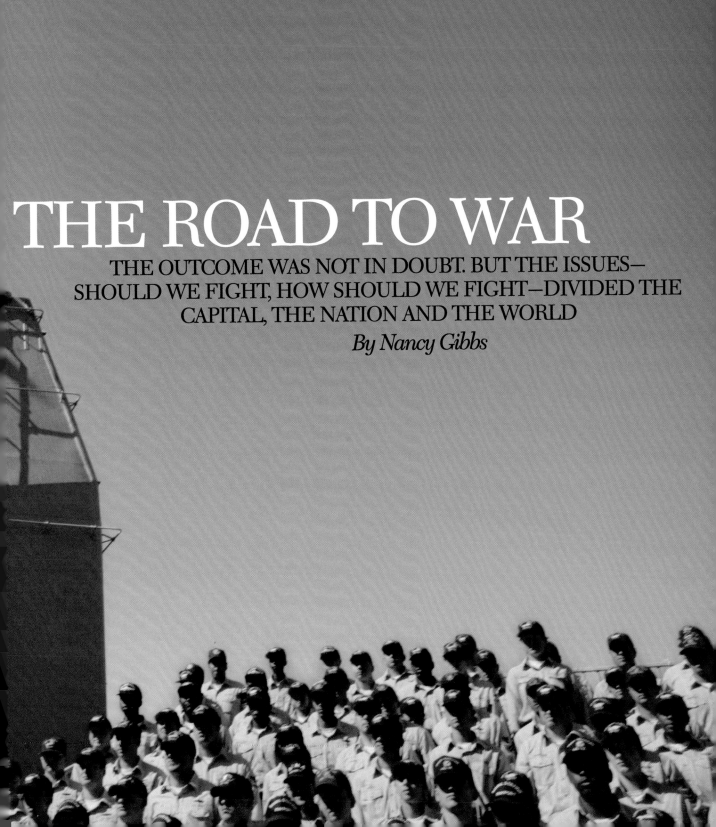

THE ROAD TO WAR

THE OUTCOME WAS NOT IN DOUBT. BUT THE ISSUES— SHOULD WE FIGHT, HOW SHOULD WE FIGHT—DIVIDED THE CAPITAL, THE NATION AND THE WORLD

By Nancy Gibbs

America has never thought of itself as a country that goes looking for a fight. By tradition we are reluctant warriors, who respond to a sudden siren or a shot

or to the danger of a slow, rolling storm that allows no shelter. Seldom has war come because we decide to call it, in the belief that it might be safer to fight than not to.

As the conflict drew near, George W. Bush stood before 8,000 sailors in Jacksonville, Fla., and

U.N. Friends Urge The U.S. to Wait

The Security Council, led by France, Germany and Russia, would not support a war resolution and pleaded for more time and inspectors. The U.S. and Britain were now on their own

declared that "the terrorists brought this war to us, and now we're taking it back to them." And 21 days after it began, the war was over. In front of another crowd of sailors, this time on the U.S.S. *Abraham Lincoln,* he reduced the war with Iraq to one battle in a larger and still unfinished War on Terror, and while "we do not know the day of final victory ... we have seen the turning of the tide." Victory in Iraq

came so suddenly that it was easy to forget the recent warnings: the Arab world would boil with resentment, emboldening terrorists; Middle Eastern allies would fall because America was going to war on terms never tested before in our history. At different times the Administration advertised its message as a search for weapons of mass destruction, a regime change for a captive region and a hunt for terrorists and those who might help them. For once, foreign policy set off a passionate debate in America's kitchens and classrooms, in the streets, in the press and the pulpit, accompanying those in Congress and at the U.N. Security Council. Seldom in recent history had the whole country, the whole world laid out the values that should guide a nation's actions and tried to rank them in order of merit. How much was America's security truly threatened by Saddam Hussein's regime? What price would be paid for the precedent of pre-emptive war? What actual or moral authority should the U.N. claim? What damage would be done to a frail U.S. economy? Would it be possible

to target Saddam yet spare his people from harm?

Those questions inspired the largest antiwar demonstrations in a generation, as protesters from Calgary to Copenhagen denounced America as the greatest threat to world peace. But people struggled with the issues privately as well. By the middle of February, as the autumn consensus in the Security Council to press for Saddam's disarma-

Prayers in D.C., Stares in Baghdad
Bush, top center, prays before beginning a Cabinet session as war draws near. In Iraq, soldiers kept close tabs on U.N. inspectors, who did not find much in the way of either banned weapons or cooperation

Peace Advocates Turn Out in Force

This antiwar march in Chicago was one of many staged worldwide. Millions of protesters rallied in London, Paris, Rome and New York City in the largest antiwar protests since the Vietnam era

Photograph by
Anthony Suau

> "God will roast their stomachs in hell at the hands of Iraqis!"
>
> **MOHAMMED AL-SAHHAF**, Iraq's Minister of Information, predicting the fate of coalition forces

Getting Outfitted And Outraged

A man peruses the racks of military uniforms, above, in a shop in Baghdad as war draws close. Five days before bombs drop on the capital, demonstrators brandish guns and slogans

ment gave way to a bitter fight over whether anything short of war could achieve that outcome, the American public was showing the strain. The U.N. fight weighed heavily, partly out of sentimental faith in the principles of international cooperation but also out of a hardheaded conviction that America didn't need any more angry enemies.

The country had been one big neighborhood-watch group for the 17 months since 9/11. But Feb. 7 was only the second time the terror-alert level had reached code orange, and Administration officials privately put the odds of a major terrorist attack in the next couple of weeks at 1 in 2. Rumors were viral, spreading by word and wire; a friend called a friend to say her ex-boyfriend's sister's friend's father was a top New York City cop and had told his daughter to "avoid the subway for the next 36 hours." Parents sent their kids to school that week with valentines and laminated emergency-contact lists. They added duct tape and plastic sheeting to their shopping lists.

In that context, the prospect of war was all the more alarming. Forty-eight percent of people surveyed in a TIME/CNN poll believed that war would make another terror attack more likely. Sixty-one percent thought war would weaken the economy. By the time the war was just a month away, a narrow majority, 54%, favored removing Saddam by force—a level comparable with that before Gulf War I. Women had more misgivings than men, African Americans more than whites, Democrats and independents more than Republicans. Beneath those predictable patterns, pollsters

detected deep reservations about the pro-war arguments and strong personal connections to the President who was making them.

As the diplomatic and domestic fights unfolded, Defense Secretary Donald Rumsfeld would spend hours at his stand-up desk in the Pentagon, poring over a secret document known as Deployment Order No. 177, which detailed exactly when, how and where Army and Marine battalions, Navy carrier groups and Air Force fighter wings were to be deployed for war in Iraq. As much as this was to be Bush's war, it was Rumsfeld's as well, a mirror of a different battle he had been waging with his military chieftains over the future of the U.S. armed forces. General Tommy Franks would run the campaign as head of the U.S. Central Command, and it was the general who actually prepared the plan. But as a Pentagon officer noted at the time, "That misses the point. Franks may be the draftsman, but Rumsfeld's the architect."

Generals, and their civilian partners, are not exactly expected to broadcast their battle plans. But in this new war of pre-emption, the first battle

was psychological: scare the enemy enough, and maybe you shorten the fight. By February the promise of an aerial assault that would inspire "shock and awe" in the regime in Baghdad was a staple of Pentagon briefings. But America's overwhelming air superiority masked an argument over how many ground troops would actually be needed, what role the special-operations forces would play and, above all, how exactly would an

Faith in the Face of a Coming Storm
Worshippers gather at al-Kadhimiya Shi'ite shrine, above, in mid-March. Below, women touch the door and door knocker of the shrine's mosque

PHOTOGRAPHS BY JAMES NACHTWEY—VII

Vowing Ultimate Loyalty To a Doomed Regime

Iraqi martyr volunteers parade in Baghdad just before the war. They were as good as their word. Some of the fiercest fighters proved to be Syrians, Yemenis and other Arab jihadists

Photograph by Yuri Kozyrev

> ## "Try to imagine having 20,000 soldiers pick up and move out in a three-week period. It's a lot more complicated than it looks. You got to get your lawn service done, get your pet taken care of, close out your rent, turn off your cable and phone."
>
> **COLONEL LOUIS WEBER**, 3rd Infantry Division, Fort Stewart, Ga., on the everyday logistics of preparing to go to war

PHOTOGRAPH BY MARK RICHARDS

Parting from the Ones Who Matter

Captain Stanley Echols of the 270th Military Police Company of the National Guard gets some send-off quality time with his wife Denise and their children. He is also vice principal of a California middle school

invading force of 200,000 Americans, along with 45,000 British fighters, topple a regime?

In the main, Rumsfeld wanted a faster, leaner fighting force than Franks and the generals thought necessary. The Defense chief believed that Iraq's army was far weaker than it had been 12 years before. He wanted the air war and ground war to begin almost simultaneously, compared with the 39-day bombardment that preceded Gulf War I. He wanted the 3rd Infantry Division to steam headlong for Baghdad west of the Euphrates, straining its supply lines in hopes of overrunning the Iraqi Republican Guard. The 3rd I.D. would eventually meet the Marine 1st Division and the 101st Airborne taking the central route up the Tigris-Euphrates valley, while the 1st

Marine Expeditionary Force and British forces would secure Basra and the oil port of Umm Qasr. Although Turkey declined to host an invasion of northern Iraq, special-ops forces integrated with Kurdish militia there months before the fighting began. Special-ops teams also laid the groundwork for securing the precious oil fields and limiting Saddam's ability to use his worst weapons.

It was a bold strategy that promised both greater risks and greater rewards. "Rumsfeld wanted to do something more innovative than have a quarter-million armor-centric troops marching up the Tigris-Euphrates valley," said Brookings Institution military analyst Michael O'Hanlon. The final battle plan landed somewhere between Franks' vision and Rumsfeld's, with a

Catching the
Red-Eye for Kuwait
Members of the 101st
Airborne Division from
Fort Campbell, Ky., embark
for war in early March. The
highly mobile Screaming
Eagles figure prominently
in the Pentagon's
preference for tactical
speed over massed armor
and infantry
Photograph by
Benjamin Lowy—Corbis

larger force than the Secretary envisioned but a faster attack plan than ever tried before.

As the French and Germans played out the drama in the U.N., logistics magicians were shipping more than 380,000 tons of cargo to the Persian Gulf, a volume that demanded as much deck space as 230 Wal-Marts. Soldiers knew they were moving out soon when they got word to switch from their forest-green to their desert-tan uniforms. An army of seamstresses sewed flags and patches on crisp new sleeves; new fathers paced the living room with restless babies, breaking in their desert boots.

Not since Desert Storm had the Army's entire 3rd Infantry Division, some 20,000 soldiers and support personnel, been ordered to move out en masse, like a whole town emptying in a matter of weeks. For the company commanders, the last-minute training picked up as the clock ticked down: make sure every soldier is qualified on his weapon (meaning he can snap shoot a quarter-inch hole in a target the size of a soccer ball, or a human head, at 100 yds.). Make sure the right equipment is shipped. Make sure everyone has their teeth checked and prepares a will. There were countless checklists. Do you have your canteen, Kevlar vest, decontamination kit and then the really important stuff the older soldiers told you to be sure to pack: extra socks, clothespins, Twizzlers, toilet paper, extra-thick boot insoles? Liquid laundry soap, because the water will be cold. Extra thermals, because the nights will be too.

Because the Army is now more than ever a

family business, there was an army of moms shipping out, about to learn what it really means to balance job and family under extreme circumstances. Those who had husbands staying behind found themselves conducting a crash course in smooth braids and matching clothes. "I gotta tip my hat to women," said Robert Ward, 31, a father of three, as his wife shipped out from Fort Campbell in Kentucky. "I didn't know it was so hard. Really hard." Deploying parents made recordings of their children's favorite books for the kids to listen to while Mom or Dad was gone. Potential parents hurriedly hitched: in Hinesville, Ga., business at the justice of the peace was up 77%.

As for the troops already in the theater, there were ever more anxious moments, gas-attack drills, urban-combat training and low-flying practice sorties. There were moments for more personal preparation: a last-minute baptism in the desert, a last letter home before mail call was left behind. And, as in every war, boredom—in the near 100°F heat. A few bedraggled Iraqi soldiers came to the border and tried to surrender, but they were told they would have to wait until the fighting started.

When the war began at last, on a hunch, with the bombing of a high-command bunker, one kind of tension finally eased but was replaced by another. "On your young shoulders rests the fate of mankind," Marine commander Major General James Mattis told his men—which may have been a weighty reminder, but at least it meant it was time to go do their job. And they knew that the sooner they got it done, the sooner they would be heading home. ∎

A Spiritual Pause Before Battle
Marines kneel during a Sunday Mass offered by a Catholic priest at a 1st Marine Division camp, the northernmost U.S. base in Kuwait

Photograph by
Robert Nickelsberg—Getty

Bombs over Baghdad
The U.S. ultimatum to Saddam Hussein to step down had barely expired when President Bush ordered a bombing raid to take out the Iraqi dictator. The decapitation strike was followed by a storm of Tomahawk missiles and bombs on the capital that set government buildings ablaze along the Tigris River. Gulf War II was under way

Photograph by
James Nachtwey—VII

21 DAYS
TO BAGHDAD

The warning to Saddam Hussein was stark. Surrender in 48 hours or your regime is history. He didn't. It is. In Operation Iraqi Freedom, American and British forces, aided by Kurdish militias, overcame the Republican Guard, fedayeen fanatics, fierce sandstorms and second-guessing from Stateside to conquer Iraq's army in just three weeks. From Kuwait to Kirkuk, here is their story

From Kuwait, All Roads Lead North

A convoy of U.S. Army 3rd Infantry Division armored vehicles waits to depart for its attack position along the Iraqi border. Unlike the battle plan for Gulf War I, this time ground and air attacks were to be launched almost simultaneously

Photograph by Christopher Morris—VII

The Biochem Fear:
"Gas! Gas! Gas!"

The cry goes up among the 101st Airborne near the Iraqi border in Kuwait. As sirens warn of incoming missiles, soldiers fumble into biochem suits and cram into a bunker. Iraqi rockets either missed or were destroyed; none carried gas warheads

Photograph by
Benjamin Lowy—Corbis

The Steel Wave Gets Rolling

The Marines' strategy was to overwhelm the Iraqis with speed, men and armor. Yet until this day, most had never been in battle

NEAR BASRA

"Multiple Iraqis in the quarry with weapons," said the voice over the radio. "And they're not surrendering." It's 4 p.m. on the first day after the initial air assault on Baghdad. For hours I've traveled north across the desert with the Marines of the 3rd Battalion, 4th Marine Regiment, 1st Marine Division. Packed tightly into an amphibious assault vehicle— Marines call it an amtrac—we head toward our destination, just outside the strategic city of Basra in southern Iraq. The mission will

be to cut off troops of the Iraqi army's 51st Division. But first we found ourselves in an old stone quarry, miles from Basra, that had become a refuge for Iraqi soldiers. Not long after we arrived, two appeared in the open and headed on foot toward one of the amtracs.

At first the Marines thought the pair was about to surrender—until they opened fire, that is. Instantly a Marine sniper climbed to the top of our amtrac and lined up a shot, but the two men darted behind the cover of a sandy berm. Moments later, Sergeant Major David Howell, using an amtrac for cover, sneaked up behind the soldiers

as they came out to surrender and forced them to the ground.

What these young Marines— many of them barely out of their teens—are discovering is that real-life enemy terrain is not quite like the models on which they trained. A miniature Iraq, built in the sand at their camp in Kuwait, had towns that were small patches of red buildings with Iraqi soldiers represented by black-and-white targets. Now the towns are real and populated by flesh-and-blood Iraqi soldiers ready to kill.

Earlier in the week, whoops of delight went up as the Marines heard President Bush give Saddam Hussein 48 hours to capitulate. With that, the men began making final preparations. Most of them had already "sanitized" their packs, leaving behind photos and letters from home—anything that

"UP TO NOW THE BIGGEST KNOCK THEY'VE EVER TAKEN IS BEING TURNED DOWN FOR THE PROM"

Churning Sand and Blasting Tanks

Perched atop their amtracs, members of the 1st Marine Division watch Iraqi tanks burn, 16 miles south of Basra. Gaining control of Basra's airport and oil fields was a key early objective

Photograph by Robert Nickelsberg

could be used against them if they were taken prisoner. Some, though, hid pictures of wives and girlfriends in their gear.

After Bush's speech, as they were about to move out, their battalion commander, Lieut. Colonel Bryan McCoy, addressed them: "Demonstrate to the world that there is no better friend and no worse enemy than a U.S. Marine." He added, "We've got a very grim job ahead of us, gentlemen. If the Iraqis try to fight, we'll slaughter them. This is not going to be a fair fight."

McCoy acknowledged later that the moment was probably overwhelming for some of his young Marines. "Up to now," he said, "the biggest knock they've ever taken is being turned down for the prom. I don't think they understand yet the combat capabilities they possess. But they will once they start attacking."

We did not move into Iraq until this morning. Yesterday was marked by frequent gas-attack alarms, always false but each of them requiring us to rush into our chemical suits. Last night, bedded down in sleeping bags on the desert floor, we could hear the huge rumble of U.S. artillery pounding Safwan Hill, just over the border. Sometime around 1 a.m., we were awakened and began to pull out.

Hours later we were on the road, packed into the amtrac, 16 in the back, with a crew of three in front to drive and act as shotgun. We reached the Iraq-Kuwait border very quickly, though most of us could not see much. One of the Marines shouted up to Lance Corporal Tyrell Joyner, 19, who

was posted up top, "How does Iraq look?" Joyner shouted back, "Like Nevada! There's sagebrush and stuff!"

Making swift progress, we passed about a dozen Iraqi POWs sitting on the ground cross-legged, with their hands behind their heads. Elsewhere we passed the adobe houses of villagers who were out working in their well-watered gardens. As our convoys drove past, many of the villagers stopped to wave. The young Marines were moved. It was their first encounter with Iraqi civilians, and they had not been sure what to expect.

The next day we headed for Basra International Airport, which the Marines were to secure, when we were almost hit by what appeared to be a tank round. Fortunately, we had learned that the Iraqis are not very good at redirecting fire once they have nearly hit a target. Two Marines prepared to fire a shoulder-launched multipurpose assault weapon, a rocket that can take out a tank. As they stepped out, another enemy round went off. Missed again. We drove on.

By the time our vehicle got to the airport, having been delayed by a broken fuel pump, Basra International was held by Marines. The battle for the airport—McCoy would later describe it as "brutal"—was over. Before they fled, the Iraqis had set fire to the airport administration building and had strewn the runway with debris to prevent U.S. planes from using it. All that remained was a statue of a waving Saddam standing forlornly amid the wreckage. **—By Simon Robinson**

> "My fellow citizens, at this hour American and coalition forces are in the early stages of military operations **to disarm Iraq, to free its people and to defend the world from grave danger.**"
> —GEORGE W. BUSH, announcing that war had begun in Iraq

> "**The criminal little Bush** has committed a crime against humanity."
> —SADDAM HUSSEIN, in a speech televised soon after the first missile strike on Baghdad

> "Regardless of the duration of this conflict, it will be fraught with **consequences for the future.**"
> —JACQUES CHIRAC, President of France, who strongly opposed the war

> "It is time for us to realize that the **liberation** is under way, and it **is inevitable.**"
> —COLIN POWELL, Secretary of State

> "They lack any kind of courage. They literally hide behind women and children, holding them in their houses as they fire… **They really lack manhood.** They're violating every sense of decency. They're as worthless an example of men as we've ever fought."
> —MAJOR GENERAL JAMES MATTIS, 1st Marine Division commander, on tactics employed by Iraqi paramilitary fighters

Sources: www.whitehouse.gov; Reuters; New York Times; NPR; Washington Post

DAY 2 Making New Friends, Cadging a Meal

Iraqi boys greet Marines who have just entered Safwan, in southern Iraq. Some troops carried spare rations for humanitarian aid. Others doled out candy or sliced open their own MREs, handing over a meal ready to eat to the hungry

Photograph by Christophe Calais—In Visu/Corbis

DAY 3 At Nasiriyah, the War Moves Indoors

Rifles high, members of the Army's 3rd Infantry Division are ready for anything as they clear a building in Nasiriyah, site of one of the fiercest early fire fights. Soldiers went door to door to root out fedayeen forces

Photograph by Christopher Morris—VII

DAY 3

A Target for Both Sides

A man suspected of being an Iraqi soldier is taken into custody by the 3rd Infantry. Many Iraqis doffed their uniforms and surrendered if they could. But Saddam's loyalists employed execution squads behind the lines to deter defections

Photograph by
Christopher Morris—VII

**Breakfast with
Light Armor**
Members of the 3rd Infantry
Division pause for a meal
after parking their Bradley
fighting vehicles near
Nasiriyah. The Bradleys,
along with M1 tanks,
provided the Army with
devastating superiority
against Iraqi armor

Photograph by
Christopher Morris—VII

A Soldier Attacks His Commanders

Early on, the 101st Airborne Division suffered casualties from within. Paratroopers at Camp Pennsylvania in Kuwait carry a comrade wounded after grenades were tossed by an American soldier

Photograph by Benjamin Lowy—Corbis

Attack from Within

TIME's Jim Lacey was with the 101st Airborne Division's 1st Brigade when one of its soldiers attacked a command tent

NORTHERN KUWAIT

It was 1:45 in the morning when I was awakened by the first blast—a boom 10 times as loud as a car backfiring. Ten seconds later there was a second blast, and then soldiers started screaming, "Get out! Get out!" Someone had tossed three hand grenades into the tent housing more than a dozen of the brigade's officers. One woman in my tent, which was 10 yards away from the explosion, yelled, "I'm hit!" A piece of shrapnel from the grenade had lodged in her leg.

I ran out of my tent into total chaos. The Scud alarms were sounding, and people were running for the bunkers we use dur-

ing those alerts. Most soldiers were in uniform, but some were wearing the workout clothes they sometimes sleep in. Realizing the explosions were not Scuds, I walked over to the tent where the grenades had gone off and saw two very badly hurt soldiers—one bleeding from his leg, back and stomach. I noticed the chaplain trying to comfort the dozen or so who had been hit. Sergeants were shouting orders to form a security perimeter. Some of the younger soldiers were looking on in a state of shock and had to be hand-led to their positions. Fifteen minutes later an ambulance drove up to take away the badly wounded. One died soon after from a gunshot to the back—a soldier said the assailant had been lying in wait by the tent entrance with a

rifle. (A second officer would die two days later from his wounds.) Because a number of officers had been hit, no one knew at first who was in charge. Then two officers who were bleeding from wounds started giving orders.

Thinking there was a terrorist on the loose, a group of soldiers began assembling to con-

Exploding Grenades in the Officers' Tent

Soldiers asleep in Camp Pennsylvania in northern Kuwait knew the enemy lurked nearby. They could not have imagined that he would be one of them. Soldiers guard two Arab workers, top left, but it was Sergeant Asan Akbar—seated, below left—who was charged with killing two Americans and injuring 14, one of whom is shown being treated

Photographs by Benjamin Lowy—Corbis

duct a manhunt. Other officers were inspecting the tents and bunkers to make sure everyone was accounted for.

One of those officers spotted a soldier, lying alone in a bunker near the explosions, who appeared to be wounded. The soldier had, according to military sources, recently been acting insubordinate; his superiors had decided not to bring him into Iraq.

He initially admitted responsibility, camp sources say. The officer drew his weapon and called for backup. Then they handcuffed the soldier, read him his rights and waited for criminal investigators to arrive.

The soldier was later identified as Sergeant Asan Akbar, 32. He was charged with two counts of murder and 17 counts of attempted murder (14 of those at the scene were hurt; three were unharmed). The grenade attack killed Army Captain Christopher S. Seifert and Air National Guard Major Gregory Stone. Akbar has said his attack was in response to harassment by other soldiers over his Muslim faith. He was taken to Fort Knox, Ky., on charges that could bring the death penalty if he is convicted. ■

DAY 4

Frantic Search for a Phantom Flyer

In the reeds along the Tigris River in central Baghdad, Iraqis armed with guns, knives and anger search for a reportedly downed U.S. pilot. Three American jets were shot down over Iraq in differing circumstances— but none over Baghdad

Photograph by
James Nachtwey—VII

DAY 4

Less-Than-Precise Devastation

This house in northern Baghdad was destroyed by an explosion, possibly from a U.S. cruise-missile attack. Although missiles with satellite-guidance systems were delivered with great accuracy, some are believed to have gone astray

Photograph by Yuri Kozyrev

Making an Unscheduled Stop

In Samawah, Iraqis wait by the road after members of the U.S. Army's 3rd Infantry Division stopped the bus they were traveling in. The men aboard were searched for arms or other evidence of military involvement

Photograph by
Christopher Morris—VII

DAY 6

Here's Sand in
Your Eyes ...

And your gun and your pack
and your boots. The three-
day sandstorm didn't stop
the fighting, but it did alter
tactics. Here, members of
the 1st Marine Division
slept and snacked on
Skittles while their vehicle
waited near Nasiriyah

Photograph by
James Hill—Getty

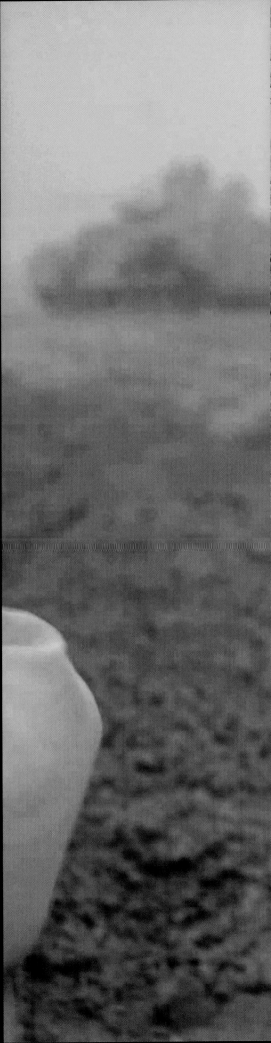

DAY 6

Essential Question:
Friend or Foe?

With every civilian now a potential combatant, a sandstorm that stopped the convoys in their tracks only complicated the issue of friend and foe. In this encounter, soldiers of the 3rd Infantry Division questioned and frisked three people who turned out to be just what they appeared to be—two adult civilians and one very frightened little boy. Civilians who didn't understand or heed warnings to stop were often fired on

Photographs by
Christopher Morris—VII

DAY 6

Downtime in Downtown Baghdad

Baath Party members on guard in the sandstorm-hued city catch up on the news. Initially, coalition forces didn't target the capital's main television transmitter. But persistent appearances by Saddam Hussein changed that strategy

Photograph by Yuri Kozyrev

DAY 7

Failed Ambush
On the Road

A slain Iraqi lies near a highway in central Iraq, where he and others attacked a Marine convoy. These tactics forced commanders to move more units from the front lines to guard the supply convoys but did not halt the march on Baghdad

Photograph by
James Hill—Getty

The Highway Of Destruction

The infiltration by fedayeen into southern cities made coalition forces adjust their battle tactics

NAJAF

The 2nd Brigade of the 3rd Infantry Division planned to halt west of the city; it also planned on facing some resistance from local irregulars. What it didn't expect was a rush-hour-like Iraqi attack, the road dense with enemy trucks bearing down on the brigade. "My headquarters had just rolled into the objective area when 10 pickup trucks loaded with men firing machine guns and RPG-7s came racing down the road," recalls Colonel David Perkins, commander of the 2nd Brigade. "My lead tanks blew up the first three vehicles, but the rest kept coming. It was the start of a long night."

For hours, the Iraqis continued this furious drag race—floor it and fire—whipping down the road from Najaf into the waiting guns of the 2nd Brigade's M1 Abrams tanks. The M1s obliterated them. So while the attacks had a high nuisance value, they were unable to do any damage to the 2nd Brigade. Nor did the timetable to Baghdad slow down. Says Perkins: "I didn't expect this many of them, but all that meant was we used up more ammo. And I have plenty of that, especially if it means not fighting these guys in Baghdad."

Iraqi irregulars have tried everything to get at 2nd Brigade soldiers. When two Bradley fighting vehicles got stuck in the mud, dozens of irregulars, armed with a machine gun and TOW missiles, tried to crawl up to them. Another Iraqi group attempted to paddle across the Euphrates River, shooting rocket-propelled grenades as they approached. Their five boats were blown apart in the water. All these attacks ended similarly. "It's not a fair fight," says Major Kevin Dunlop. "Trucks with machine guns against tanks and Bradleys can only have one outcome. We are slaughtering them."

On the other side of the Euphrates, east of Najaf, the 7th Cavalry ran into an even bigger fight. This time the main attack came during a swirling dust storm that made thermal night sights useless. Iraqi irregulars swarmed around the U.S. forces. The Americans were ordered to stay put and shoot at anything that moved. By midnight, it was over. Two U.S. tanks were disabled, blasted from behind, their most vulnerable spot, by antiaircraft guns mounted on pickups.

strike on a fedayeen stronghold.

By the next morning, Perkins estimates, his unit had killed more than 1,200 attackers and taken the fight out of the rest. At first light, an Iraqi colonel walked up to an American position and surrendered. "He was a POW in the last Gulf War, so he had practice in surrendering when things are going bad," says Captain Cary Adams. The Iraqi colonel said he had only 200 of his 1,200 men left and claimed that originally there had been two other brigades in the town. One moved out during the night toward Baghdad, he said, while the other was hunkered down in government buildings around the city.

As the Iraqi attacks died down, the 101st Airborne Division began arriving to release the armored units for other missions. Brigadier General Benjamin Freakley, assistant division commander of the 101st, briefed the leaders of the companies that would be encircling Najaf. Everyone expected the remaining fedayeen to attempt a break toward Baghdad, even if it meant running the 101st's gauntlet. But some of the fedayeen were likely to stay and conscript the locals at gunpoint again. Freakley prepared his men to face a moral conundrum. Said

As a result of the M1s' unique armor, no one on either tank was injured. And one of the tanks was recoverable.

The next rush-hour attack came right after dark the following day, but by this time, the 2nd Brigade had set up "tollbooths"—heavy armor—on the roads leading from Najaf. "They attacked like morons," says Perkins. "But they kept coming." In one area guarded by two Bradleys, several hundred Iraqis were killed, according to the local battalion headquarters.

Dunlop thinks the Iraqi brigade that moved out to the north was the one the Air Force had reported engaging, and he does not believe there is much left of it. As for the brigade that is still waiting in the city, no one is in any hurry to go in after it. "We are here to liberate Najaf, not to get into a street fight there."

So if the 2nd Brigade had taken the fight out of the enemy,

what provided it in the first place? And does a town that is putting up so much resistance really want to be liberated? The short answer is yes. Civilians continually wandered out of town to encourage and even beg the U.S. soldiers to take Najaf. They said fedayeen irregulars were forcing local members of the al-Quds militia to fight by gathering their families together and threatening

to shoot them if they did not oppose the Americans. At one point, locals came out to thank the Americans for killing the area's Baath Party leader, who, they said, had been executing civilians. The Baath leader, they said, had been killed in an air

he: "Imagine someone walking into your home and saying either you fight, or we will kill your wife and daughters. They are doing what any man would do to protect his family." It wouldn't be easy killing men who were doing that. —*By Jim Lacey*

"TRUCKS WITH MACHINE GUNS AGAINST TANKS AND BRADLEYS CAN ONLY HAVE ONE OUTCOME."

DAY 8

Taking Shelter from The Coming Storm

Kurdish refugees from the village of Chamchamal in northern Iraq abandoned their homes, fearing an Iraqi attack. Many Kurds who lived near areas controlled by the Iraqi government sought safety in the mountains during the war

Photograph by
Kate Brooks—Corbis

HIGH-TECH FORCE

APACHE LONGBOW
The newly modified Apache can use its radar systems to detect and classify more than 120 targets, identify the 16 most dangerous, transmit that information to other aircraft and begin an attack—all in less than 30 sec.

Pilot

Co-pilot/gunner

Up to eight Hellfire missiles under each wing

Pilot's night-vision sensor

30-mm chaingun

In the Air
No Iraqi aircraft rose to challenge the coalition's control of the skies. Iraq's air defenses were largely confined to ground fire, without the radar guidance that would have triggered certain destruction from precision weaponry. Coalition bombers and fighters were able to operate freely. Still, low-flying, slower helicopters were vulnerable

Dahuk

Tall 'Afar

Mosul

I R A Q

Tikrit: Saddam's hometown; last major city to fall

Euphrates River

Anah

Hadithah

THE WAR

Facing overwhelming firepower on the ground and deadly precision from above, Iraqi forces largely melted away in the face of the coalition onslaught, mounting only pockets of tough resistance

H2 Airfield

H3 Airfield

Rutbah

Special forces seized two strategic airfields that Iraq could have used to launch Scud missiles at Israel

JORDAN

The Push To Baghdad
Unable to use Turkish bases to launch a northern front into Iraq, U.S. forces moved north from Kuwait, battling ambushes from Saddam's irregulars while crushing Iraqi army units. Meanwhile, British forces besieged Basra, Iraq's second largest city. In northern Iraq, U.S. special forces helped Kurdish fighters gain control of key cities, tightening the pressure on the Iraqi regime

On the Ground
The tens of thousands of troops that streamed across the Iraqi desert toward Baghdad relied on the most advanced armor and artillery in the world: self-propelled howitzers that can hurl shells 19 miles; mobile launchers that fire 12 surface-to-surface rockets in less than a minute; high-tech personnel carriers; and tanks that travel faster than 40 m.p.h.

M1 ABRAMS
With thermal imaging, night vision, laser range finders and computerized targeting, this is the world's most advanced—and most lethal—tank. But it uses nearly 2 gal. of gas to go a mile

ID panel: Shows as a "cold spot" in other U.S. tanks' thermal imaging to prevent friendly fire

.50-cal. machine gun

Gunner's primary sight

7.62-mm machine gun

120-mm gun

TIME Graphic by Ed Gabel, Joe Lertola and Jackson Dykman

Sources: *The Illustrated History of McDonnell Douglas Aircraft;* GlobalSecurity.org; Lockheed Martin; Defense Department

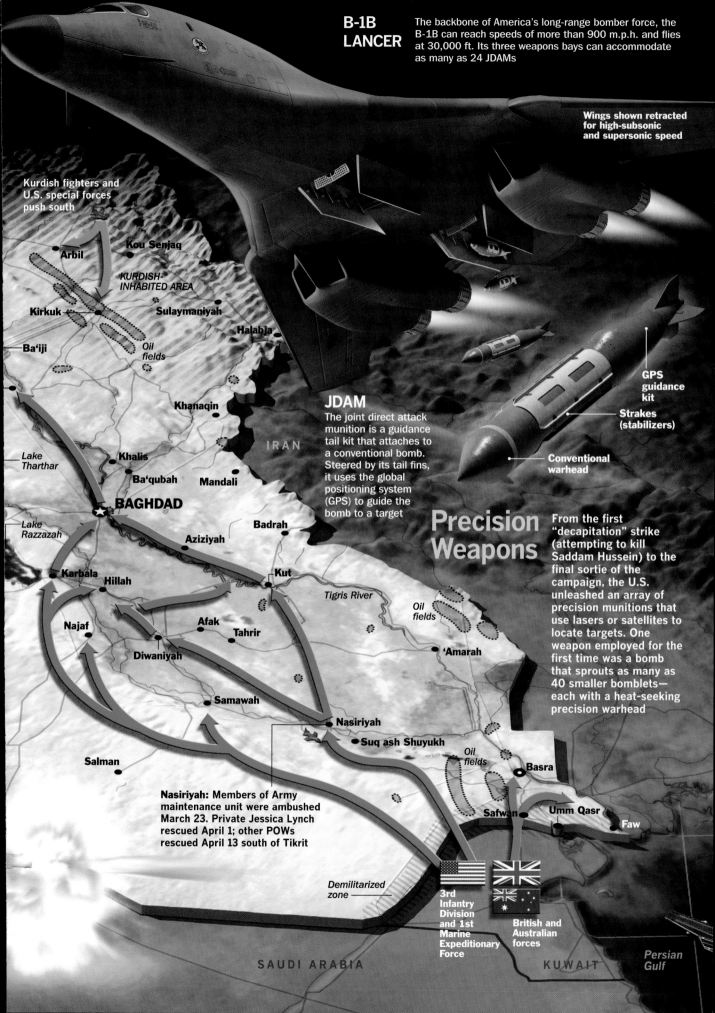

B-1B LANCER

The backbone of America's long-range bomber force, the B-1B can reach speeds of more than 900 m.p.h. and flies at 30,000 ft. Its three weapons bays can accommodate as many as 24 JDAMs

Wings shown retracted for high-subsonic and supersonic speed

Kurdish fighters and U.S. special forces push south

Arbil
Kou Senjaq
KURDISH-INHABITED AREA
Sulaymaniyah
Kirkuk
Halabja
Ba'iji
Oil fields
Khanaqin

IRAN

Lake Tharthar
Khalis
Ba'qubah
Mandali
BAGHDAD
Lake Razzazah
Badrah
Aziziyah
Karbala
Hillah
Kut
Tigris River
Najaf
Afak
Tahrir
Oil fields
Diwaniyah
'Amarah
Samawah
Nasiriyah
Salman
Suq ash Shuyukh
Oil fields
Basra

JDAM
The joint direct attack munition is a guidance tail kit that attaches to a conventional bomb. Steered by its tail fins, it uses the global positioning system (GPS) to guide the bomb to a target

GPS guidance kit
Strakes (stabilizers)
Conventional warhead

Precision Weapons

From the first "decapitation" strike (attempting to kill Saddam Hussein) to the final sortie of the campaign, the U.S. unleashed an array of precision munitions that use lasers or satellites to locate targets. One weapon employed for the first time was a bomb that sprouts as many as 40 smaller bomblets—each with a heat-seeking precision warhead

Nasiriyah: Members of Army maintenance unit were ambushed March 23. Private Jessica Lynch rescued April 1; other POWs rescued April 13 south of Tikrit

Demilitarized zone

3rd Infantry Division and 1st Marine Expeditionary Force

British and Australian forces

Safwan
Umm Qasr
Faw

SAUDI ARABIA

KUWAIT

Persian Gulf

BAGHDAD

Saddam Hussein had vowed a bloodbath for U.S. forces entering his capital, home to more than 5 million Iraqis. But after weeks of precision bombing, Baghdad's defenses—and Saddam's regime—crumbled quickly

Saddam Grand Mosque *(under construction)*

Central railway station

National Parliament

Mutanabbi

Mansur Street

Grand Mosque *(under construction)*

Mansur

Ministry of Oil

Zawra Park

Baghdad fairgrounds

Dimashq Street

Zaytun Street

BAGHDAD PRESIDENTIAL COMPLEX
Palaces and government buildings are concentrated in this zone

✴ Known targets of bombing

Intelligence Services headquarters

Harithiyah

Kindi

Parade ground

Telecommunications center

Arts center

Clock tower

al-Salam Palace

Baath Party headquarters

al-Sijood Palace

Qadisiya Expressway

SCOTT NELSON—GETTY

Passport control

INTERNATIONAL ARRIVAL: U.S. soldiers make their way through the main terminal of Baghdad's airport

U.S. FORCES took the airport before moving into the sprawling, densely populated capital

Saddam City

B A G H D A D

Area of photo

Rasheed Airport

Khanazir Island

Tigris River

International Airport

4 miles
4 km

Jami'ah

Jadriyah Bridge

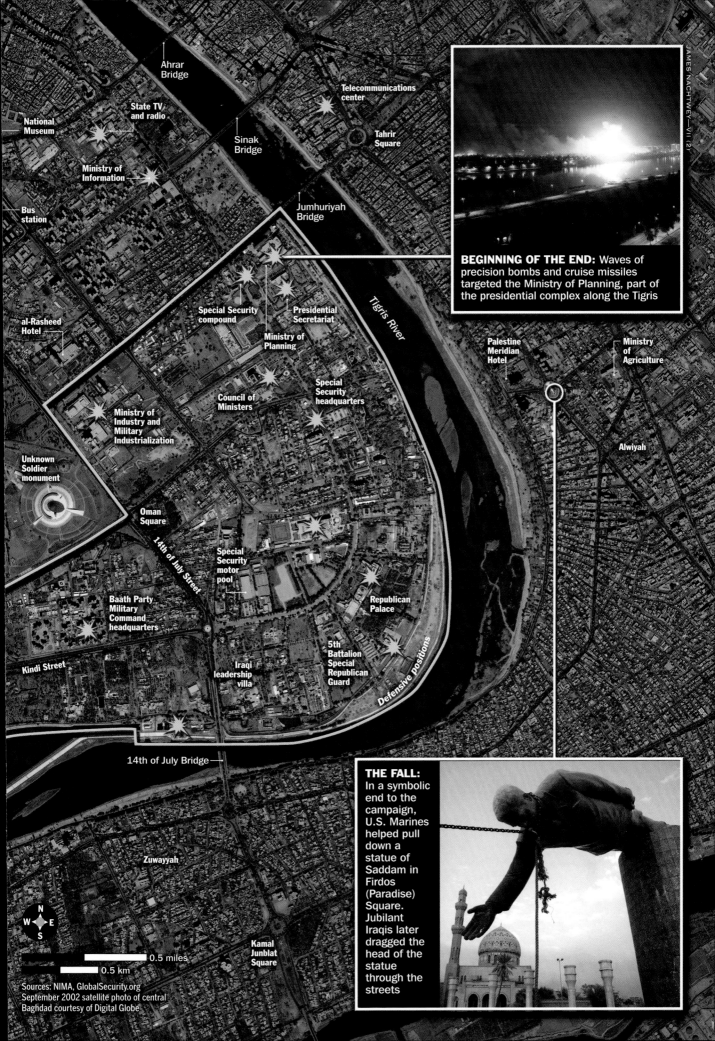

Ahrar
Bridge

State TV
and radio

National
Museum

Ministry of
Information

Sinak
Bridge

Telecommunications
center

Tahrir
Square

Bus
station

Jumhuriyah
Bridge

Special Security
compound

Presidential
Secretariat

Ministry of
Planning

al-Rasheed
Hotel

Tigris River

BEGINNING OF THE END: Waves of
precision bombs and cruise missiles
targeted the Ministry of Planning, part of
the presidential complex along the Tigris

Council of
Ministers

Special
Security
headquarters

Palestine
Meridian
Hotel

Ministry
of
Agriculture

Ministry of
Industry and
Military
Industrialization

Alwiyah

Unknown
Soldier
monument

Oman
Square

14th of July Street

Special
Security
motor
pool

Republican
Palace

Baath Party
Military
Command
headquarters

Kindi Street

Iraqi
leadership
villa

5th
Battalion
Special
Republican
Guard

Defensive positions

14th of July Bridge

THE FALL:
In a symbolic
end to the
campaign,
U.S. Marines
helped pull
down a
statue of
Saddam in
Firdos
(Paradise)
Square.
Jubilant
Iraqis later
dragged the
head of the
statue
through the
streets

Zuwayyah

N
W · E
S

0.5 miles

0.5 km

Kamal
Junblat
Square

Sources: NIMA, GlobalSecurity.org
September 2002 satellite photo of central
Baghdad courtesy of Digital Globe

On the Wings of Falcons

Coalition forces ruled Iraq's skies using an array of air power that kept Iraq's jets grounded and its antiaircraft defenses nearly mute

DOHA

Air Force Sergeant Stephen Albano, a jet mechanic, saw a dozen airmen sprinting toward the runway of the coalition air base where they work. He took off too, worried that something had gone terribly wrong with one of the planes stationed there. Others from his crew joined in, but suddenly the 25 men came to an abrupt stop at the edge of the runway. One started waving an American flag. A second began flailing his arms wildly. Only then did

Albano, 36, get it: nobody had been injured. Instead, it was just an adrenaline-filled send-off for an F-16 Fighting Falcon on its way to Iraq. "We may not be on the front lines, but we're a part of a team," said Albano, a 17-year aircraft-maintenance veteran.

The pre-emptive airstrike launched by carriers and cruise-missile-carrying submarines and destroyers that got Gulf War II off to an unanticipated early start began what Brigadier General Rick Rosborg—the air base's commander and head of the 379th Air Expeditionary Wing—called "perhaps the greatest concentration of air power in the history of warfare." Much of that firepower emanates from this installation near Doha, Qatar. Here more than 5,000 servicemen and -women launch more than 100 aircraft each day, delivering tens of thousands of pounds of bombs on Iraqi targets.

Americans Above, Destruction Below

Iraq had no answer to U.S. air superiority. Al Rashid Communications Center in Baghdad was destroyed in a missile attack

Photograph by James Nachtwey—VII

One part of this aerial effort is the 22nd Expeditionary Fighter Squadron, attached to the 379th, operating in near secrecy in Doha. The unit, whose motto is "First In, Last Out," is the successor to the Vietnam-era Wild Weasels, the daring flyers whose job it was to be sitting ducks to draw enemy gunfire and then attack the air-defense systems. "We don't run from enemy fire," says Lieut. Colonel Grant Bishop, a silver-haired 40-year-old who has been flying F-16s for 12 years. "We turn in to it and go one-on-one."

Although the U.S. rules the skies—not a single Iraqi fighter has risen to meet an American warplane—the pilots say there has been plenty of ground fire on many missions. The key factor as far as they're concerned is that the Iraqis are not turning on their radar systems, which would provide guidance for their missiles. But the radar would also identify the antiaircraft launchers to F-16 pilots. Instead, the Iraqis are basically firing into the air. "That proves to me these guys are being made to shoot," says Captain Chris Vance, 27. "They know if they lock on to us, we'll destroy them."

The unit has not lost a plane, a remarkable record when the air base is launching so many flights a day, each of which can last up to eight hours. The F-16 is one of the military's most versatile planes, used for everything from attacking missile batteries to providing close air support for B-2 bombers. The F-16 pilots have ranged across Iraq, bearing down on targets in dozens of the so-called kill boxes, the 30-sq.-mi. grids that the coalition uses to map the country. The fact that no Scuds have hit neighboring countries speaks to the effectiveness of the F-16 crews. "Think of us as snowplows," says Vance. "We're just clearing out the threats."

It takes scores of people to get a single F-16 aloft. Sergeant Chandra Kirby is a "life-support specialist," whose job is just what her title implies. She is responsible for making sure each element of a pilot's survival equipment is working and pre-pared, from the oxygen mask to the parachute. She has had to scramble to set up workstations in her tent, bending hangers into hooks and using makeshift lockers to save the precious equipment from the ever present sand. "I know a pilot's life depends on how well I treat this," Kirby, 29, says as she gently cradles one of her pilots' helmets.

There are other delicate jobs: Sergeant Marcus Hankins assem-bles bombs. For days before the air war kicked off, he and his team were attaching guidance systems and tail fins on a convey-or line that could take a few hours for each 2,000-lb. bomb. The key responsibility for Hankins, 31, though, is to avoid "paperweights." That's the term pilots use for a dud—and it's Hankins' job to find out why a munition didn't explode, which hasn't happened much.

But the dark reality of duds and misguided bombs hangs over a pilot. There are long target lists that the pilots methodically work their way through. "I triple-check my targets," says Colonel Bishop, "and before I hit the 'pickle' [the red weapons-release button on the sidestick], I think, and think again. The possibility of civilian casualties is always on my mind." The father of a 14-month-old daughter, Bishop says he has seen the pictures of the dead U.S. soldiers and dead Iraqi chil-dren. "Those are all emotional images for us, and we do every-thing we can to protect our own and protect innocent civilians."

There have been mistakes: it was an F-16 that destroyed part of a Patriot missile battery. And the job is getting tougher as the U.S. troops swarm Baghdad. "There used to be plenty of dis-tance between the enemy and us," says Captain James Caplinger, 27. "Our world is getting smaller—and more chal-lenging." And because of Caplinger and crew, Saddam Hussein's regime was shrinking as well. —*By Sally B. Donnelly*

A One-Two Punch From the Air

Naval aviators joined Air Force pilots in bombing and surveillance missions over Iraq. Here, a crewman from the U.S.S. *Constellation* helps launch an F-18

Photograph by Robert Nickelsberg—Getty

"THINK OF US AS SNOWPLOWS," SAYS VANCE. "WE'RE JUST CLEARING OUT THE THREATS."

F-16 pilots from the 22nd Expeditionary Fighter Squadron at their air base near Doha, Qatar

KAREN BALLARD—CORBIS

DAY 9

**Packing Heat in
Saddam's Honor**

**Tribal chiefs and sheiks
from villages throughout
Iraq came to Baghdad for
instructions on carrying out
guerrilla warfare in their
provinces against invaders.
This leader, who arrived in
a private car, brandishes
his weapon on a city street**

Photograph by
Yuri Kozyrev

DAY 9

Grieving for a Bombing Victim

An Iraqi mourns a relative killed in a blast at a suburban Baghdad market. Locals blamed U.S. bombs, but the Pentagon isn't certain. The number of civilians who perished isn't known. But most accounts put the tally in the thousands

Photograph by
James Nachtwey—VII

DAY 10

Sharing the Grief for A Loved One Lost

A woman hands prayer beads to a man as they mourn a family member killed in an explosion at the city market on the outskirts of Baghdad. Iraq blamed the U.S., but American sources raised the possibility of an errant Iraqi missile

Photograph by
James Nachtwey—VII

Commandos Prowl the Peaks

In northern Iraq, U.S. special forces have a task similar to what they did in Afghanistan: to eliminate Islamic terrorists

HALABJA

The battle rages, fierce and bloody, perhaps the heaviest fighting northern Iraq has seen so far. U.S. special forces are here, along with their Kurdish allies, facing down Ansar al-Islam, the die-hard terrorist group based in Kurdish-controlled Iraq that the Americans believe is linked to al-Qaeda. "There are three or four isolated pockets of Ansar on very high ground. We're closing in on them from everywhere we can," says an American commando named Mark, who declines to give his rank or last name. All afternoon the Ansar fighters rain down sniper and machine-gun fire from a craggy peak high above the Americans. From the flat plains about two miles below, pro-American Kurds return the favor with artillery.

Positioned on a mountain-side in between, the Americans unleash their own barrage. During four hours of battle, I saw U.S. forces drill Ansar with mortars, heavy machine-gunfire and antiaircraft artillery, 40-mm grenades and 500-lb. bombs dropped from planes overhead. Still, their fire was answered by an enemy clearly visible through binoculars. At one stage an Ansar defender screamed, "God is great!" even as grenades and heavy rounds peppered the cave he had ducked into.

Special-forces marksmen joined the battle. Three of them took positions behind a rock, patiently waiting to kill their Ansar counterparts far above. "There's a sniper playing with us," said one U.S. soldier. The Americans' high-powered rifles cracked intermittently. When the incoming rounds finally ceased, the Americans picked themselves up. "I think between us we smoked three guys, sir," one said. "Oh, at least," added another.

It was the latest in a running battle waged since Ansar had been driven from its front line in the lowlands. A day earlier,

"I THINK BETWEEN US WE SMOKED THREE GUYS, SIR," ONE SAID. "OH, AT LEAST," ADDED ANOTHER

Iraq's Other Tyrants Get Theirs

Kurdish troops and U.S. special forces stand over a dead Ansar al-Islam fighter, left, while a Kurdish soldier, below, continues the pursuit in the mountains near Iran. The radical Islamic, al-Qaeda-allied band persecuted Kurds and Sufis in northern Iraq in any village they took over
Photographs by Kate Brooks—Corbis

about 100 U.S. soldiers had joined with Kurdish *peshmerga* (those who face death) in an assault against Ansar's base. The U.S. bombs flattened a mosque in the village of Biarra that had been used as terrorist headquarters, replete with a gun pit on top. The assault capped a week of pummeling by American Tomahawk cruise missiles that prompted the militants to take to the snowy mountains

bunkers; others were cut down as they fled over open ground or among relatively exposed rocky outcrops. Their corpses remained where they had fallen throughout the assault.

In the end, however, the battle for Halabja seemed inconclusive. President Bush last week referred to the destruction of Ansar's base as one of the war's important early achievements. But it may be a limited

bordering Iran. This corner of northeastern Iraq, near the town of Halabja, is rough territory, a no-man's-land of escape routes and caves impervious to all but the mightiest bombing.

The assault clearly took a toll on Ansar's radical followers. Politburo member Mahmood Sangarwi of the pro-American Patriotic Union of Kurdistan says 60 dead were left behind after yesterday's battles. In the rocky terrain of today's exchange, I saw eight more slain Ansar fighters. Some had died in their

one. In Halabja, U.S. commando Mark says, "A lot of the senior cadre fled a long time ago, leaving a fanatical hard core to stay for the last stand. They had little intention of surviving." The Americans blasting away at the holdouts recognize this and lament opportunities lost. "This is my second time in northern Iraq," says a special-forces soldier. "I should be in Tampa with my wife enjoying spring break. Instead I'm here, and I wouldn't be if we'd done this right the first time." —*By Michael Ware*

VERBATIM

"We will use any means to kill our enemy in our land, and we will follow the enemy into its land. This is just the beginning. You'll hear more pleasant news later."
—TAHA YASSIN RAMADAN, Iraqi Vice President in Baghdad, referring to the suicide attack that killed four U.S. soldiers at a security checkpoint

"I'm an American soldier too."
—PRIVATE JESSICA LYNCH, prisoner of war, from her hospital gurney in Nasiriyah, to U.S. commandos who had burst in to rescue her

"For the first time in my life, I feel free."
—BASSAM SALAH MADLOOL, nine-year veteran of the Iraqi army, deserting his post just south of Kirkuk to surrender to Kurdish militia

"It is purely a case of shaping the battlefield, getting our troops equipped and in the right place for the next part of the campaign."
—CAPTAIN AL LOCKWOOD, spokesman for coalition forces in Qatar, denying there was any order for an "operational pause" to delay the push toward Baghdad

"I am still in shock and awe at being fired."
—PETER ARNETT, in his debut column for London's *Daily Mirror,* after he was let go by NBC for appearing on Iraqi TV and calling the coalition's war plan a failure

Sources: Chicago *Tribune;* L.A. *Times;* A.P.(2); *Daily Mirror*

DAY 12

Taking a Breather
Before the Big Push

The Marines raced toward
Baghdad on a route that
generally followed the
Euphrates River. This young
Marine and his buddies are
dug into a position not far
from Hilla, a river town
about 65 miles south of
their ultimate objective

Photograph by
James Hill—Getty

A Military Target's Collateral Damage

An Iraqi laments the loss of a home that stood across the street from a Baghdad telecom center bombed by U.S. forces. Although the U.S. tried to avoid damage to civilian areas with precise bombing, that wasn't always the case

Photograph by James Nachtwey—VII

DAY 12

A Coffin's Traces
Of Tragic Cargo

A cemetery worker returns
from the funeral of an
Iraqi woman killed by
an explosion in fighting
south of Baghdad. He is
hoisting the coffin used to
transport the victim to her
grave site. It would be
needed for other funerals

Photograph by
Yuri Kozyrev

HOME FRONT

War's arrival brought out anxiety and passions among Americans. Were we in the right? Would our homes be safe? How many casualties? TIME photographer ANTHONY SUAU documented the conflicting emotions he witnessed while traveling the U.S. as the war unfolded

Although many citizens had misgivings about starting a war with Iraq, support for the war effort built quickly, as in this rally on Capitol Hill, once hostilities began

SUPPORT MY DAD I DO!
AMericA & Britain all the way

A young boy voices his opinion at a pro-military rally in the nation's capital in support of the more than 300,000 military members in the gulf. In some places, dueling pro-war and antiwar demonstrators faced off

W*ith three cable-news networks fighting for ratings, Gulf War II was the most intensely covered conflict in history. Among the vantage points: a hotel bar in Charlotte, N.C.; Times Square in New York City; and a family restaurant in Elizabeth City, N.C.*

"Support our troops, deplore our policy" became the motto of many antiwar protesters in communities across America. Demonstrations were staged in most major cities before and during the war, including these pictured in San Francisco and Chicago

The Pentagon's strategy tried to minimize CASUALTIES, but that effort could

not begin to compensate the communities and families that would suffer painful loss

The war came home to La Harpe, a small farming community in west-central Illinois, when word was received that one of its own, Marine Corporal Evan James, had been killed in action in Iraq. On the main street, a local fire fighter clutched the large flag that would soon be displayed in the town square to honor the young Marine. James was given a hero's funeral, with Marine honor guard, which took place at the local high school gym, a location big enough to contain the outpouring of mourners

Into the Fire with the Marines

Portrait of a battlefield commander: a TIME correspondent takes a wild ride into battle with an aggressive Marine officer

DIWANIYAH

Having carefully brushed his teeth, checked his ammunition and then looked over a map with his men, U.S. Marine Lieut. Colonel Bryan McCoy, 40, announces the day's activity as if he were running a fishing club. "We're going chumming," he announces. "We're going to throw some bait into the water and see if the sharks will come out."

The sharks are an estimated 3,000 Iraqi soldiers in Diwaniyah, a city of 300,000 people 110 miles southeast of Baghdad, where the 1991 southern Shi'ite rebellion against Saddam Hussein started.

The Marines are the bait. It seems like a dangerous tactic, even though the Iraqis are out-gunned. But McCoy's battalion is hanging back in order to clear out pockets of resistance and secure supply lines. "We want to keep the enemy on their heels," he says. So as the rest of the 7th Marine Regiment pushes north toward the capital, the 3rd Battalion, 4th Marines, attached to the 7th Regiment in Iraq, plans to pick a fight at the rear of the convoy. "It's just a good opportunity to kill these guys," McCoy says. "I don't say that with a lot of bravado, but we're here to break their will. I don't want to sit on our asses all day with the enemy just over there."

As a rooster announces daylight, battalion vehicles line up along the highway, pointing in every direction so as not to give away the point of attack. Then the tanks, amtracs and humvees head west toward the outskirts of Diwaniyah.

The chum is now in the water, and the Iraqis rise immediately to take it, pinging the Marine armor with small-arms fire. A tank crewman answers, firing his coaxial machine gun into an enemy bunker. Over the radio comes a play-by-play: "Yeah, baby," says a voice. "He just ate coax for breakfast," says another. The sharks are already on hand when the Marines arrive, and the Iraqis seem to fill up the palm-studded field in front of the Americans. McCoy calls for artillery support as his men fire TOW missiles.

The Marines are now spilling out of amtracs and charging at the Iraqis. The idea is to push the infantry out quickly enough to stop the enemy from establishing bases of fire. It's a tactic McCoy deployed successfully just days ago in a battle at nearby Afak and one that defines him as a commander. "Go in there as if you own the place," he says later. That sense of supremacy now takes the form of artillery shells that are pounding Iraqi positions. Another TOW missile hits a large building, which sheds dust as if someone had beaten it with a stick.

The Marines reach the edge of town, and small groups of Iraqis surrender. An old man strips off his jacket and waddles toward a Marine position in a dirty white singlet. "There are militia on every corner in the city," he says, unfolding a story now familiar in the Shi'ite south. "They

Planning to Get into Harm's Way

Marine Colonel Steven Hummer, center, and Lieut. Colonel Bryan McCoy, left, plot strategy near Kut. Their tactic is to stick their necks out to flush enemy troops and then overwhelm them with firepower and attitude

Photographs by Robert Nickelsberg—Getty

tell us to fight or they will kill our children. They say if we are captured, the U.S. will tie us up and leave us in the desert, and when Saddam returns, he will kill us."

McCoy and his humvee team—a driver, a gunner, a radio operator and a TIME correspondent—drive across a scrub-filled field and stop on a small dirt patch between two bunkers. McCoy jumps out and shoots into the bunker on his side of the humvee. His gunner takes the other. Both turn out to be empty. But McCoy's aggressiveness is classic Marine, and the men like it. "He's the first one into battle and the last one out," says a Marine. "He's not like other battalion commanders, sitting in their humvees at the back." And McCoy clearly revels in being a warrior. "I'm in my happy place," he says.

The tank company pushes through the field, flushing out the enemy and destroying two "technicals"—white pickups, one with an antiaircraft gun and one with a machine gun mounted in the back. The tanks hold the east of the city, while the infantry pushes up from the south toward the tanks. The battalion skirts the city's edge. The Marines don't want to be drawn into street fighting, and it appears that dozens of Iraqi soldiers managed to withdraw into the city. Still, the chumming gambit is a success for the Marines. They have killed 92 Iraqis and taken 44 prisoners, and not one Marine has been injured. Says McCoy: "Let's quit pussyfooting around and call it what it is. It's murder, it's slaughter, it's clubbing baby harp seals."

The next time could be different, though, and McCoy knows it: "As casual as we talk about it, taking human life is not to be taken lightly. Without getting all heavy and syrupy about it, it's a big deal. Sooner or later they're going to get one of us, or

"LET'S QUIT PUSSYFOOTING AROUND AND CALL IT WHAT IT IS. IT'S MURDER, IT'S SLAUGHTER."

two of us, or five of us or more. It's just not our time yet. But odds are, it's going to happen."

Two days later, in fact. Fresh from battle, McCoy's unit reverses course and heads east, crossing the Tigris over a bridge captured earlier by another Marine battalion. We pass under the gates of Kut and into the town. To the north of the road is open ground, surrounded by houses. To the south, a large palm grove, thick with grass.

Suddenly, gunfire rings out. "Baynes, Baynes, 3 o'clock!" shouts McCoy to the gunner atop his humvee. Small-arms fire pesters the convoy from the palm grove and buildings to the southeast. A rocket-propelled grenade hits the side of an armored vehicle. The Marines pour out of their amtracs and charge into the grove, driving forward, taking bunkers, hiding behind berms. A Marine goes down, a kid, a bullet through his gut. Bullets fly over the hood of McCoy's humvee. For a few minutes this grove seems like the hottest place on earth. There is smoke and explosions

and bullets and cries.

And then it is over. The Marines push through, destroying weapons, capturing prisoners. An injured Iraqi soldier is dragged up to the road, his right leg twisted at the knee so that his foot faces backward. Another lies down next to me. "Don't kill me," he says in English. "Please, I can't fight. My arm, don't twist it left or right. It's broken." The Marines have destroyed 10 tanks and 14 antiaircraft guns and, they say, killed 78 Iraqis. As the Marines withdraw from town, thousands of Iraqi civilians, mostly men, are waiting at the gates to go in, as if they were working in a factory, taking over for the death shift.

The Marines have suffered one dead and three wounded. By the scorecard of battle, that's a huge victory, but "all that is not worth a Marine's life," says McCoy. "These are my boys. They did it for me. I went to the injured, and they said, 'We got them, sir.' They're still seeking approval even then. They're good kids. Only they're not kids anymore." —*By Simon Robinson*

Some Old-Fashioned Leathernecking

Once in the midst of the enemy, Marines come pouring out of their amtracs to concentrate fire on Iraqi positions. The Marine above carries a SMAW (shoulder-launched multipurpose assault weapon). On this day, the battalion kills many Iraqis but also discovers Syrians and other Arab fighters among the dead

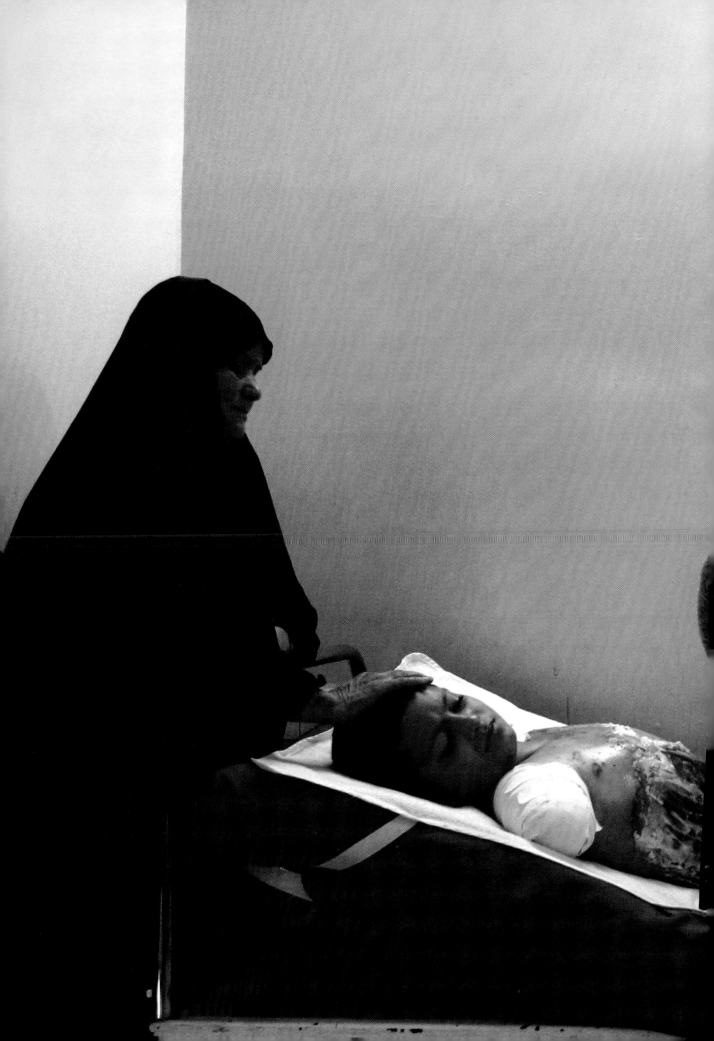

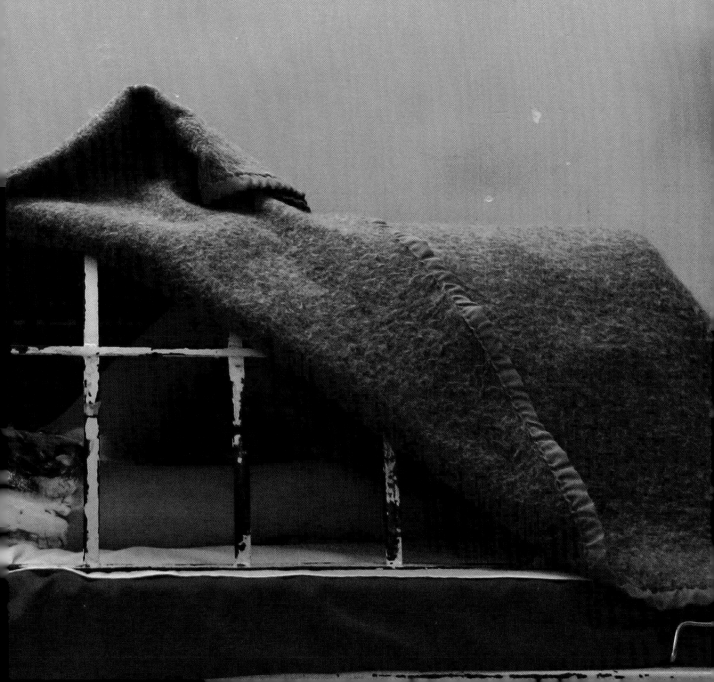

DAY 13

The World Embraces A Wounded Boy
Ali Ismail Abbas, 12, was sleeping at home when the missile struck. His mother, brother, sisters and stepfather died; he lost both arms and was severely burned. After TIME ran this picture, offers of aid came pouring in, enabling him to be moved to a hospital in Kuwait for treatment

Photograph by Yuri Kozyrev

DAY 13

An Air Show Erases Saddam's Defenses

With Baghdad's air defenses wiped out and the Iraqi air force absent, U.S. jets could concentrate on precision strikes against government targets. The bombs were generally accurate; some citizens felt safe enough to be on the streets during an air attack

Photograph by Yuri Kozyrev

DAY14

A Farmer Dies, and a
Soldier Laments

"It bothers me to hell that
the guy is innocent," said
the sergeant whose men
killed this farmer when his
truck did not stop at a
checkpoint. U.S. troops
became extremely wary after
a suicide bomber north of
Najaf killed four Americans

Photograph by
Christopher Morris—VII

DAY 15

The Remains of a Day of Combat

The deadly detritus of war litters the desert floor following the battle for the town of Aziziyah, an oil outpost southeast of Baghdad. An oil refinery smokes in the background, but most of Iraq's energy infrastructure was spared

Photograph by
James Hill—Getty

The Soldiers Carried Smiles

The U.S. expected Shi'ites in the south to welcome its troops with open arms. Things did not quite work out that way

NAJAF

It may have been the most unusual directive of Gulf War II. "Soldiers of 2nd Battalion," ordered Lieut. Colonel Chris Hughes. "Smile!" With that, infantrymen of the 101st Airborne Division, armed to the teeth, began flashing their choppers at a crowd that had grown restless as the soldiers approached the mosque at the Tomb of Ali in Najaf, one of Shi'ite Islam's holiest sites. The days of cautiously advancing— sometimes fighting house to house, sometimes guided by civilians who pointed out the positions of Saddam's men—the Division's 1st Brigade gained control of the area. The fifth day Najaf had the feel of a liberated city. Smiling citizens crowded every street around the American positions. There was a constant stream of people willing to give information and loudly condemn Saddam. American soldiers who a day before had been in close combat were now basking in the cheers and applause, their arms tired convinced that Saddam could not reach back and hurt them, as had happened after Gulf War I. "All they ask is, When will the Americans kill Saddam?" said a Kuwaiti translator traveling with the 101st. "They say it over and over, as if I did not hear them. I tell them that the Americans will kill him and not to worry."

But the euphoria was almost lost over the mosque incident. It began when the local imam, who had spent 20 years under house arrest until the city fell and his captors fled, asked American soldiers to protect him and the mosque. He neglected to explain this, however, to the crowds outside. As the soldiers of Bravo Company of the 2nd Battalion, who had formed a tight perimeter on the street, began heading toward the mosque, citizens started shouting and moving forward. With rabble rousers (later identified by Iraqis as Baath Party members) shouting, "The Americans are storming the mosque," the crowd began to chant and shake their fists. That's when Hughes made his move. Grabbing a microphone, he calmly announced over a loudspeaker, "Second Battalion soldiers, take a knee and point your weapons at the ground." Seconds later every one of the men was on a knee, and not a single weapon was pointing at the crowd. Then he gave the smile order.

It worked. Hughes kept his men like that for about five minutes and then returned to the microphone. "Soldiers of the 2nd Battalion, we are going to stand up and then walk slowly back to base. You will not point any guns at the crowd, and you will smile at everyone." A minute later the Smilin' Second was walking away from the mosque, and the Iraqis

The Message: We'll Finish the Job

The leader of the local Iraqi Freedom Forces talks with Brigadier General Benjamin Freakley. Since their revolt was crushed a decade ago, Shi'ites were wary of their liberators. Assured that Saddam was no longer a threat, they became more cooperative

Photograph by
Benjamin Lowy—Corbis

tactic helped win over a crowd that had more questions than answers. Were the soldiers going to storm the mosque, as some agitators were shouting? Were they liberators? Or conquerors? Were they really going to kill Saddam Hussein this time?

Najaf's civilians watched with hope and concern as the 101st made repeated incursions into the city, rooting out the remnants of regular and irregular Iraqi forces. After four from returning friendly waves.

There were women and children in the crowds, but only the men did any talking. They would say the word Saddam and spit. Or run up to U.S. soldiers and shout, "George Bush good!" Said Sergeant Reuben Rivera: "The American people, particularly the movie stars against us being here, need to see this. These people need us. Look how happy they are." The locals at last seemed began intermingling with them, patting them on the back and giving them thumbs-up signs again.

By midday, however, citizens began to raise more pressing concerns. People stopped praising Bush and began asking for water. The brigade brought in 1,000 gallons, but that wasn't enough to meet the need. U.S. military engineers, meanwhile, set to work to restore power and the water supply. But the people still seemed overjoyed, if thirsty. The biggest problem U.S. soldiers faced was keeping the crowds away from them as they tried to patrol the streets.

The Americans were further encouraged when a group of local Shi'ites said they wanted to join the fight against Saddam. Both sides agreed to convene at the city center, and tanks were sent to secure the area. The site, it turned out, was dwarfed by a giant statue of Saddam on horseback. Lieut. Colonel Ben Hodges, the brigade commander, got an idea. After confirming that the statue really was of Saddam, he had engineers wrap the base with explosives. Then he waited.

A few hours later about 30 Shi'ite fighters arrived. They were wearing new military vests and carrying Russian-made weapons. Not an army, said a special-forces soldier, though he added, "It's a start. Tomorrow we will have 10 times this number." The Shi'ite leader, who did not wish to be identified, was beaming as he approached the U.S. troops. He told the soldiers how he hated Saddam and how all the people in Najaf hated Saddam. He went to great pains to make clear that his was a self-financed outfit, independent of the U.S. Army. Asked the name of his group, he replied, "The Coalition for Iraqi National Unity." U.S. commanders tried

to tell him which sectors his men should avoid, fearing cases of mistaken identity. But it became apparent that the leader was in no mood to discuss technical details, and was more interested in making sure everyone understood that there was now an uprising against Saddam—and that he was leading it.

The Shi'ite leader accepted the honor of detonating the explosives ringing Saddam's statue. With a thunderous blast Najaf's most visible symbol of Saddam's regime toppled in a heap of twisted metal. People ran from the side streets cheering and climbing over the wreckage, enjoying the giddiness of the moment. One Iraqi approached Brigadier General Benjamin Freakley, assistant commander of the 101st Airborne. "Kill Saddam," the Iraqi said, and spat on the ground. Then he added, "Now we can have satellite TV." —*By Jim Lacey*

When His Heads Started Rolling

In a scene that would later be repeated all over Iraq, one of the thousands of Saddam statues, billboards, sculptures, posters and tile portraits is destroyed by locals—here with the help of a demolition crew from the 101st Airborne

Photograph by Benjamin Lowy—Corbis

"ALL THEY ASK IS, WHEN WILL THE AMERICANS KILL SADDAM? THEY SAY IT OVER AND OVER."

DAY 16

Laden with Gear
And Heading North

U.S. Marines riding on a humvee pause along their approach to Baghdad; a few hundred yards ahead, comrades engage the enemy in a fire fight. Marines often described Iraqi fighters as brave but overmatched

Photograph by
James Hill—Getty

The Kids Who Had To Die

The strategy was to bypass the cities, but in some places, fedayeen forces left no choice but to fight house to house

KARBALA

The image of the children is impossible to forget. When the fire fight broke out, all the soldiers could think of was their first casualty, Specialist Larry Brown—his side open, his eyes lulling—being carried out past them. But he was a man of 20, and he was a professional infantryman. The kids—boys—were maybe 7 or 8 and had no place there. Bravo Company wasted them. Had to. Right when the fire fight was at its hottest, when maybe 100 guys were popping up across the rooftops firing AK-47s and rocket-propelled grenades (RPGs), the boys bounced into the courtyard below the building where Bravo was spread out and attempted to retrieve an RPG dropped by a dead Iraqi. "It sounds terrible when you hear about this cold, away from the fight," said commander Lieut. Colonel Chris Holden. "We shot and killed children. But I accept full responsibility for that. That's the kind of fight it was."

It was the kind of ugly, house-to-house bloodbath the U.S. had feared most, especially in Baghdad. But it happened first in Karbala, which before Baghdad collapsed loomed as a potential stranglehold on the supply route leading to the capital. History had already stamped Karbala in blood. In A.D. 680 Muhammad's grandson Hussein and a small group of supporters fought to the death here over the right to lead the Muslim faith. Now scouts reported that 500 to 700 Fedayeen fighters—irregulars devoted to Saddam—were digging in to make a stand.

For Bravo Company, part of the 502nd Brigade of the 101st Airborne, the battle for Karbala started ahead of schedule, on the morning of April 5. Bravo was still two blocks south of its first objective, a water-treatment plant, when it began taking fire. "We were two minutes in, and we were in full contact," said Sergeant Mark de la Garza.

Taking cover behind his Bradley fighting vehicle, called Red 2, Sergeant David Brown radioed Sergeant Patrick Jarchow in Red 3 and devised a plan that would define the day. Starting from the

Taking Karbala, One Block at a Time
Helicopter assault teams of the 101st Airborne Division engage in a street fight. The soldiers, like members of other Army units, went through extensive training in urban warfare before setting out for Iraq

Photograph by Rob Curtis—Army Times/Corbis

"HE FELL AGAINST THE WALL ON HIS LEFT. I YELLED, 'GET BROWN! COVER! HE'S HIT!'"

water plant, Jarchow's men would jump from roof to roof, with Brown matching their progress on the ground, kicking in doors and clearing houses, identifying targets. Killing them.

The two squads moved steadily northeast through the city. When they reached an intersection, with both squads on the ground, Sergeant Brown pivoted left and saw a man holding two RPGs. Said Brown: "I popped two rounds at him, and I see the impact in his chest and gut. He reached down, grabbed one RPG, and it goes off and blows his foot off. The RPG ricochets and comes straight at us. We cross over the intersection, and that's when I saw Larry Brown get hit." Behind Sergeant Brown, Specialist Brown had reached the junction and was met with a short burst of waist-high fire. "He fell against the wall on his left. I yelled, 'Get Brown! Cover! He's hit!'"

Through the haze of smoke grenades, Sergeants Brown and Jarchow saw a father and daughter approach the fallen RPG gunner. Jarchow shot at the gunner again. In Sergeant Brown's words, "The girl helps him up, and they're walking away, and I popped him again, and he's down. He moves again, and I empty my magazine into him."

As the wounded Specialist Brown was helped into the back of a Bradley, the RPG gunner, to the squad's utter amazement, started to move again. "We emptied 50 rounds into him," said Sergeant Brown, "and then we shot him with a 7.62 from the Bradley. He's still talking when we leave." Not many Iraqis were. Hour by hour, enemy corpses were piling up below Bravo's rooftop perch.

Two boys were about to be added to that pile. The 3rd Platoon had been on a roof for 25 minutes when two small figures came spinning out of the court-yard, almost as if they had been pushed, and began inching toward an RPG lying in the street. "They've been testing us—getting closer to us and walking away," said Staff Sergeant James Dyer. "And the guys are all saying, 'Don't pick it up, don't touch that!' Maybe 20 or 30 guys shouting, 'Don't do it!'" A warning shot kicked up dust at the first boy's feet. He stopped and looked up: M-4s, M-16s and heavier squad automatic weapons and Bravo 240s—an entire arsenal was leveled at him.

Then, fixing the Americans with his clear, brown eyes, the boy walked forward—slowly, deliberately, defiantly—and picked up the round. "The moment he touched it, you could see a wall of lead slam into those kids," said Dyer. "It dropped the first kid immediately. The next one was hit a second later—you could see him tumble as he was running."

Eventually, after an unrelenting hour of fire and running, one squad made its way back to the water plant. The 18 wounded U.S. soldiers were evacuated by a Black Hawk that took off around 6 p.m., a full four hours after Specialist Brown had been hit. It was too late: he died soon after.

Holden said his dead opponents—279 Iraqi Fedayeen and up to 100 foreign *mujahedin*, mainly Syrians—had been the most formidable yet. "I respect them," Holden said. "They had a rehearsed plan, and they knew what they were doing." And as Karbala's ancient sand swallows this new river of blood, the men of Bravo Company will find some honor in this timeless soldiers' code of warriors well met. But as weeks fade to months, and months to years, the remembered gaze of a clear-eyed Iraqi boy is certain to linger. —*By Alex Perry*

"It is **not helpful to have those kind of comments come out** when we've got troops in combat."

—**GENERAL RICHARD MYERS,** Chairman of the Joint Chiefs of Staff, on criticism of the war plan voiced by former military leaders

"I'm a professor of national-security studies. **I know a lot more about fighting than [Rumsfeld] does.**"

—**GENERAL BARRY MCCAFFREY,** retired Army general and leader of an infantry division in the first Gulf War, who had criticized the war plan for insufficient troop deployment

"The **Americans,** bless their hearts, are fairly parochial. They **don't know anything about these countries they're dealing with.**"

—**BRUCE COLEMAN,** Londoner, comparing British soldiers with the U.S. military

"We're not softening them up. **We're killing them...** There's no way out for these guys."

—**LIEUT. GENERAL MICHAEL "BUZZ" MOSELEY,** U.S.A.F., on reports that U.S. bombers were "softening up" the Iraqi Republican Guard

"**Either he's alive and giving really bad direction to his armed forces,** or he's dead and they're making things up as they go."

—**GENERAL PETER PACE,** U.S.M.C., Vice Chairman of the Joint Chiefs of Staff, on Saddam Hussein and the Iraqi military campaign

Sources: New York *Times*; NPR; New York *Times*; L.A. *Times*; A.P.

Bringing First Aid to The Enemy

U.S. medics tend two wounded Iraqis near Baghdad. Using new techniques and equipment, U.S. military doctors were able to move advanced medical units, including operating rooms, close to the front lines

Photograph by
Christopher Morris—VII

DAY 19

A convoy from the 3rd
Infantry Division passes a
burning Iraqi tank as the
column moves deeper into
Baghdad's northwest
suburbs. The T-72 tank was
abandoned by its crew, who
knew it was no match for M-1
tanks and U.S. air power

Photograph by
Christopher Morris—VII

DAY 19

**Securing a Bridge
One Dash at a Time**

Several Marines urge their
comrades on as they take
this Euphrates crossing. It
was too damaged to carry
tanks, so they had to secure
the opposite bridgehead with
an old-fashioned charge

Photograph by Tuni
Takahashi—Boston
Herald/Reflex

DAY 19

Evacuating Wounded
After a Surprise Hit

**As U.S. Marines prepared
their assault on Baghdad,
an artillery shell made a
direct hit on an armored
vehicle. Here, a Marine
shoulders a wounded
comrade. Two crewmen
were killed, but the attack
on the capital went ahead**

Photograph by
Robert Nickelsberg—Getty

DAY 20

Sitting in a Fury,
Singing for Sanity

This bound and blindfolded
Iraqi prisoner tried to calm
himself by singing amid the
surrounding calamity. The
Marines who captured him
were attacking an industrial
complex, and their rifle fire
set some fuel tanks ablaze

Photograph by Hayne
Palmour—North County
Times/Gamma

DAY 21

A Family-Friendly Celebration

In Arbil, in northern Iraq, the arrival of U.S. forces was welcomed by the Kurds, among them a family showing off not only an infant but also an icon: Massoud Barzani, leader of one of the main Kurdish groups vying for control

Photograph by Yunghi Kim—Contact

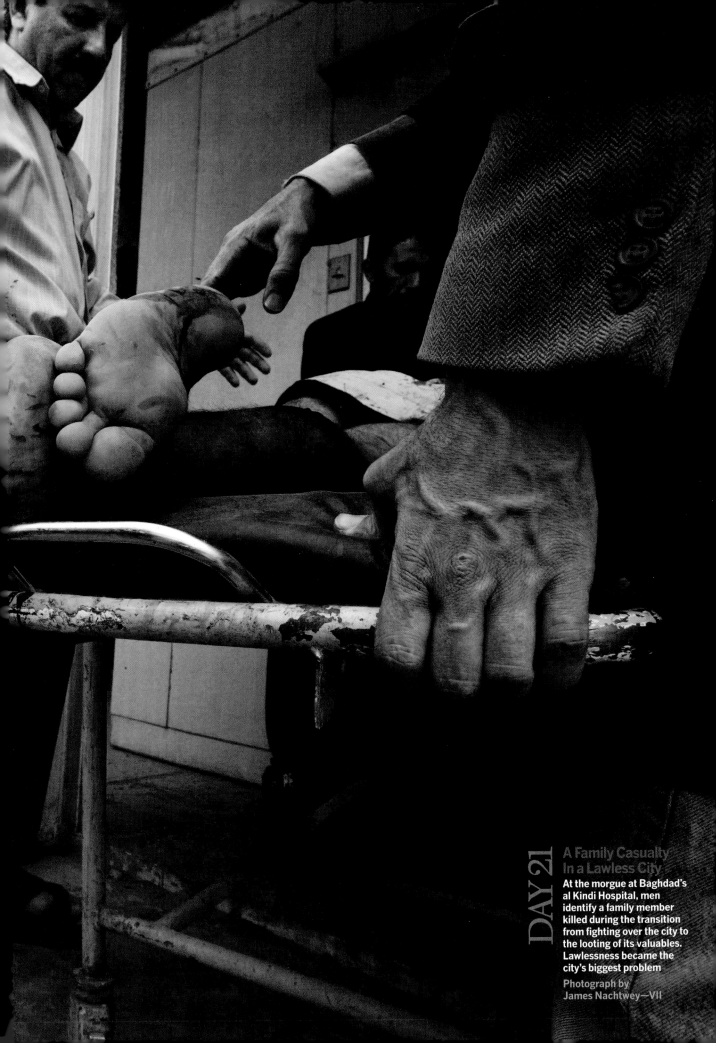

DAY 21

A Family Casualty
In a Lawless City

At the morgue at Baghdad's
al Kindi Hospital, men
identify a family member
killed during the transition
from fighting over the city to
the looting of its valuables.
Lawlessness became the
city's biggest problem

Photograph by
James Nachtwey—VII

A Statue Falls and So Does A Tyrant

After a 350-mile dash from Kuwait, the Marines were poised to enter Baghdad. A surprise was waiting for them

DOWNTOWN BAGHDAD

The plan for the day does not include anything about statues. It is simple. The 3rd Battalion, 4th Marines will rise before dawn, as they always do, and sweep forward a few miles from their overnight position in the southeast suburbs of the city. There are a few potential danger spots: an air force base, a university campus. And on an entrance ramp to the Dora Expressway, the bloated and charred bodies of Iraqi soldiers are evidence that there has recently been some resistance. But Lieut. Colonel Bryan McCoy doesn't expect too much trouble. "I don't think the enemy is going to be ready for this," says McCoy of his massed armor.

But McCoy isn't ready for what will happen either. Wednesday, April 9, is going to be a strange day. McCoy deploys his tanks and amtrac personnel carriers across three main streets and is heading north when he pulls his humvee into a small park along the central street. He has seen a blue pickup drive to a position a few hundred feet away. Is that a machine gun mounted in the back? "Twelve o'clock, Baynes. Go. Go." Lance Corporal Samuel Baynes gets his machine gun yakking on command. "I think you got him, Baynes. That guy in the back of the technical—you

shot him high and then shot him low, and he doubled over." "Yes, sir," says Baynes, a hint of wonderment and shock in his voice.

That will be the last of the opposition. As the Marines advance, the only Iraqis we pass are looters carrying mattresses, loading refrigerators onto pickups and wheeling bookcases on trolleys. Two men stroll by carrying huge sacks of soccer balls. A few people walk with their hands in the air as if to say, "Don't shoot me." Others wave white plastic bags. The message: we are peaceful. Larcenous, maybe, but peaceful.

A few hundred feet up Muasker al Rashid Street, Western journalists wander toward us. A BBC cameraman videotapes the approaching convoy. I get out of the humvee and spot TIME photographer Jim Nachtwey. He laughs, and we hug. The appearance of the press corps generates new plans. The battalion is to push deeper into central Baghdad, to the Palestine Hotel where the world's press is encamped, overlooking Firdos (Paradise) Square, the hub of eastern Baghdad.

People start lining the streets. "Welcome to Iraq," says a young boy. "Bush good." The crowd grows. There are only a few hundred people, but they are clapping and cheering more than anything this battalion has seen since entering Iraq 19 days earlier. I lean over and tell McCoy that 95% of the world press in Baghdad is in that hotel. Sadly, two journalists were killed yesterday by an American tank round from across the river. "Don't worry—we won't shoot it up," he replies. "Well, their cameras will be rolling. Perhaps it's an opportunity as much as a threat," I tell him. "Oh, yeah," he says.

As the Marine convoy pulls up to the hotel, journalists rush

our humvee. McCoy is mobbed. An Iraqi man wearing a black lounge suit pushes his way through and extends his right hand. "I am the duty manager of this hotel. Welcome to Baghdad," he says. Once the conquering heroes are hailed, the hotel man and the journalists want to know if the Marines will stay to protect them. No, McCoy informs them. He's not charged with hotel security, "but this area is now under the control of the U.S. Marines," he says.

In the square, a crowd gathers at the foot of a large bronze statue of Saddam, his right arm raised skyward as if to say, "Follow me." But now people are throwing shoes at the statue—an extreme insult in the Arab world—and a couple of men clamber up a ladder to secure a heavy rope around its head. Peace activists glare at

Where Have You Been Since '91?

A Marine in Paradise Square gets a welcoming kiss from a man in front of a soon-to-be-toppled statue of Saddam. The warmth faded when the U.S. was unable to restore order quickly

Paradise Square Gets a Retrofit

With the Marines in firm control of eastern Baghdad, citizens feel free to take symbolic revenge against Saddam Hussein. Ropes and sledgehammers soon give way to heavy equipment, courtesy of a Marine Corps tank-recovery crew

Photographs by James Nachtwey—VII

THE ONLY IRAQIS WE PASS ARE LOOTERS CARRYING MATTRESSES, LOADING FRIDGES ONTO PICKUPS

the Marines stationed around the square, who are surveying the rooftops and watching the crowd with cautious interest. Some Iraqis approach with yellow flowers, picked from a nearby garden, and hand them to young Marines. A few strap the flowers around their helmets. Iraqis laugh at the activists and human shields. "Go home," one man says to a young British woman. "You're not needed here now."

McCoy sees the large picture of Saddam above the Palestine's entrance. "I want that down," he says. A Marine points out the statue. "And that," he says. When another suggests that dismantling statues isn't part of the mission, McCoy snaps, "Get your 88 [a tank-recovery vehicle] and pull it down." Within minutes the large tow truck for a tank is driving into the square

toward the statue. At first the 88 team attaches a cable around Saddam's right leg, but it slips too low and threatens to snap when reeled in. And so, with the help of a few Iraqis, the 88 team loops a thick chain around the statue's neck. At one point an American flag is draped over Saddam's face—a photographic moment that sends the wrong message to a nervous Arab world. "It was the Iraqis' idea," McCoy says later. There is no jubilation at the sight of the Stars and Stripes but no boos either. A few minutes later the U.S. flag disappears, replaced by an Iraqi flag. Cheers go up from the people now gathered.

The 88 reverses a few feet and reels in the chain. The bronze creases at the knees and then lurches forward, Saddam's extended arm nearly touching the ground. A last tug and his knees snap and his body hits the ground and is pounced on. Later a group of Iraqis decapitates it and drags the head along the road and around the square. Much later, near midnight, I ask McCoy what he thinks of the day. "On the one hand, it's all in a day's work. It's what we train for. You need to be disciplined and not get too high or too low. On the other hand," he says, "it's not every day you liberate a country." —**By Simon Robinson**

135

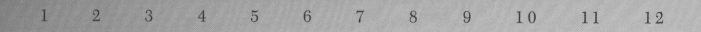

DAY 21

Yanking the Chain on Saddam Hussein

Iraq was populated with many statues of Saddam, but the one whose fall proved most symbolic stood in Baghdad's Firdos (Paradise) Square. A crowd was joined by Marines who helped pull down the statue with an armored vehicle

Photograph by
James Nachtwey—VII

Stranded In a New Regime

Saddam had displaced thousands of Kurds in the north. Now, a day after his regime lost Baghdad, his supporters had two choices: fight or flee

KIRKUK

Knowing that U.S.-led Kurdish soldiers had entered the town, Abdul Karim Hamdaniy and his son Ahmed donned plain khaki military uniforms, strapped on ammunition-filled webbing and, with Kalashnikov rifles in hand, headed out of their homes.

The faithful father-and-son team was going to die for a dying regime. "They were real members of the party, so they fought to the end," said Talat Haias, a city resident, many hours later as he stood over Ahmed's body, sprawled as though crucified in a blood-pooled halo on a suburban street. The two had taken up positions near the Baath Party center in Kirkuk's Huria district and fired at people passing by. Eventually separated, the duo

most part met no Iraqi resistance. To the east, however, it was a different story, as Iraqi soldiers tried to mount a last stand. They were positioned at the city's edge, having retreated there from bases farther afield amid intense bombing that began in March. This meant Kirkuk's first line of defense was now also its last.

When the assault kicked off, close to 300 *peshmerga* from one of the Kurds' top units raced to the Iraqi line. The fighters and the U.S. special forces leading them found themselves in a bigger battle than they had anticipated. With two tanks firing as they withdrew, the Iraqis yielded their outer ring of bunkers but stood fast on the city's outskirts. Iraqi soldier Riaz Jihad Zahir explains why he and his comrades stayed. "The officers had told us Baghdad had fallen, but they said the execution squads would kill us if we left," he says.

Five hours into the attack, the advance halted in its tracks. Around 10 a.m., the commanding team of special forces abandoned the eastern front, leaving Kurdish soldiers to hold the line. "We're going back to the 6th element. Let's go! Let's go!" shouted the team leader, waving his men into their white Land Rovers. The

Kurds began firing rockets into the Iraqi zone. Shortly afterward, a B-52 trailing four white vapors laid a carpet of perhaps a dozen bombs on the Iraqi trenches. Black clouds boiled up as the *peshmerga* whooped from their hilltop trenches that hours before had been occupied by the Iraqis being bombed. "This attack is a sacred thing," said Ismael Mohammed. He was fighting to return to the home in Kirkuk he had been driven out of seven years before. Kurdish commander Mam Rostam, a nom de guerre meaning Uncle Rostam, reveled in the momentum of the push on Kirkuk. "My soul is returning," he told his staff in the bunker.

When a second B-52 strike at last silenced their artillery, the Iraqis knew the end had come. "The officers took their uniforms off and dressed as civilians," says Iraqi soldier Zahir. "Both the Baathists and the fedayeen changed their clothes and ran off. That's when I left."

Unknown to Zahir, the mood of the city behind his sandbagged bunker had already changed. Kirkuk inhabitants say that beginning at 10 a.m., they were seeing Iraqi soldiers, paramilitaries and Baath Party members change into civvies and leave town. "Many of them gave their weapons to civilians, and they all seemed to be headed south to Baghdad or Tikrit," says Firhad Saddiq Saeed. But not all the Iraqis who wanted to leave were able to do so. Ali Hussain says he stood mesmerized as two Iraqi soldiers trying to surrender were executed by their own. "They just shot

"WE'RE HAPPY THEY'VE KILLED THEM BECAUSE THEY'VE DONE MANY BAD AND CRUEL THINGS."

hung on for about four hours before teams of Kurdish militia shot them. "We're happy they've killed them because they've done many bad and cruel things," said Haias.

The multipronged assault on Kirkuk began before daylight. U.S. special forces led battalions of *peshmerga*, as the Kurdish militia are called, who for the

order wasn't well received by all the special forces. "I'm telling you we're leaving," the leader breathlessly insisted as Iraqi artillery roared in. An argument erupted, with an angry U.S. soldier screaming, "Is this how we lead by example?" The team leader called on his subordinate to "get with the program."

Forty-five minutes later, the

them there in the street," he says.

Surprised by advancing Kurdish columns, one group fleeing the Arafa district attempted to blast its way out. A colonel among them "tried to protect himself, and [the Kurds] killed him as his men escaped," says Ramazan Miran Jwainer. Hours later, the colonel's body remained on the sidewalk, his red boots still polished, his uniform still crisply creased. Two small pockets of fedayeen diehards fought it out from a school and another building in the Wahda district. Kurdish soldiers encircled them, killing a few and capturing others. "We expect more bad things from them because they're finished and want to kill as many of us as they can," says Ghafur Salah Samin, local administrator of the Patriotic Union of Kurdistan Party.

As TIME entered the city with *peshmerga* fighters, scores of Saddam's defeated soldiers were walking the same road. None were harassed. A Kurdish radio station advised people to disarm any Iraqi soldiers they came across but to allow them to go on their way. There was at least one case of Kurdish vengeance, against a man who had killed four *peshmerga* fighters. Holed up in the Huria district Baath Party center, he had battled with Kurdish troops for hours; he surrendered in the afternoon. Burhan Mohammed witnessed what followed: "They asked him many questions, and he said he was Syrian." The *peshmerga* beat the man unconscious with rifle butts. "As he lay there, the *peshmerga* shot him," says Mohammed, "then they doused his body in petrol and burned him." Like his neighbors, Mohammed felt no pity. "They treated us like animals, so we must treat them in the same way," he says, staring down at the blackened corpse.

The vast majority of Kurds weren't out looking for blood in Kirkuk. Instead they filled the streets at midday, cheering and waving and beeping car horns. Offices of the regime's apparatus, like Baath Party compounds and police facilities, were looted and, in some cases, torched. Meanwhile, people danced in the streets, giving bouquets of flowers to U.S. special forces whose vehicles were trapped in the throng. In the center of town, a statue of Saddam Hussein was torn down. That evening happy fire from countless Kalashnikovs peppered the city's sound track. Hastily crafted THANK YOU, U.S.A. signs went up everywhere. "We are grateful to George Bush and Tony Blair," says Yaquob Yousef. "We hate not just the governments but all the peoples of Germany and France." —By Michael Ware

In the Shadow Of Death

Ahmed Hamdaniy was killed by Kurdish forces after he and his father, both Baath Party loyalists, chose to shoot it out in Kirkuk. Revenge, however, was not the rule. Although many Kurds had been exiled, their reclamation of the city was mostly peaceful

Photograph by Kate Brooks

EYEWITNESS

He was in Baghdad when the bombs began to fall and was there to meet U.S. forces as

they entered the capital. TIME photographer JAMES NACHTWEY

documents a city under siege and a people trying to regain control of their destiny

S *hi'ite women*
pray at the shrine

This American M1 tank was disabled by Iraqi fire near Baghdad, one of the few armor losses. It was then wrecked by U.S. forces to prevent the enemy from repairing and reusing it

Marines subdue a man they caught with the goods in a bank vault. Banks and museums were prime targets for looters, but hospitals and oil refineries were hit as well. The damage will stall the country's economic recovery

A criminal element plagued the historic city in the aftermath, not only looting but also attacking people on the streets or in their homes, and firing on U.S. troops. Here, a suspect is put in a headlock by a Marine

The fall of Saddam's regime leads to lawlessness and LOOTING across Baghdad
and other cities as citizens settle old scores or simply take advantage of the situation

C
onquest did not
bring an end to

الشهيد ... الثقافة صورة الميت صورته

S aying goodbye to a lost son and brother. Ali Ahmed Atti, 16, was killed in a cross fire in Baghdad. At a cemetery in Najaf, he is washed for burial by his father Ahmed, left, and his brother Mohammed

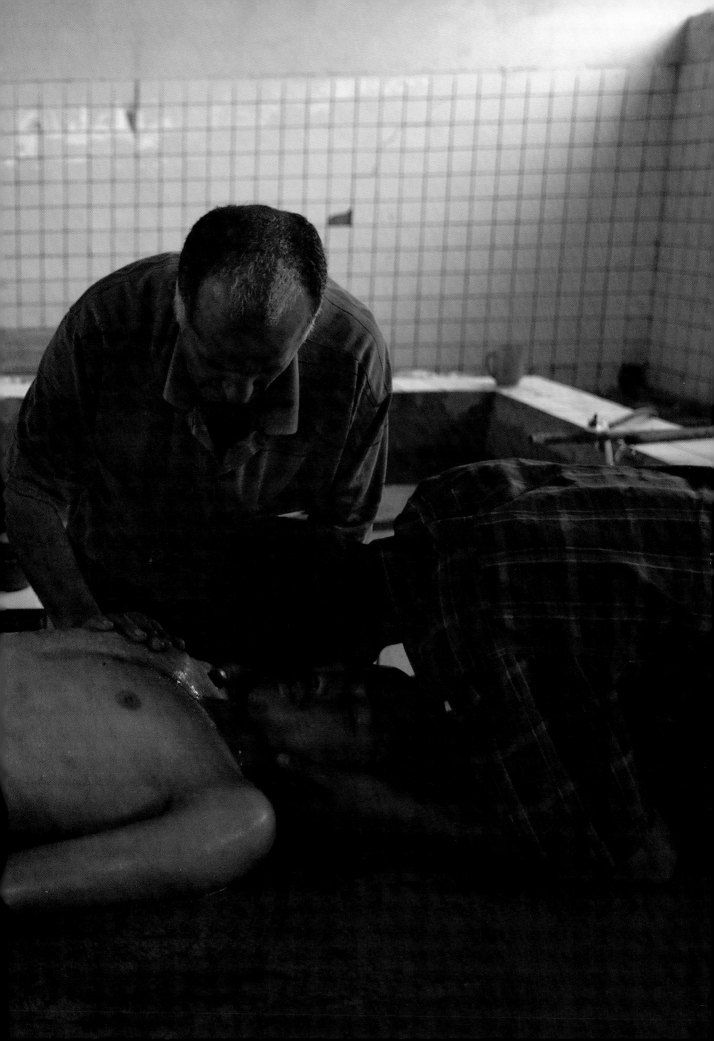

*H*e made the
ultimate sacrifice
for his country. In a cemetery
outside Baghdad, family members
gather around the coffin of their
loved one, a soldier killed by a
missile while guarding a building

F ervent, bloodied
believers cut their
scalps to honor Imam Hussein,
the grandson of Muhammad,

H uge crowds descended on Karbala from both Iraq and Iran, which, like southern Iraq, is populated mostly by Shi'ites. The site had been inaccessible to pilgrimages under Saddam

R esting place: the cemetery at Najaf, the preferred burial ground for Shi'ites, is one of the largest in the world. Many families are reburying their deceased here now that the war is over

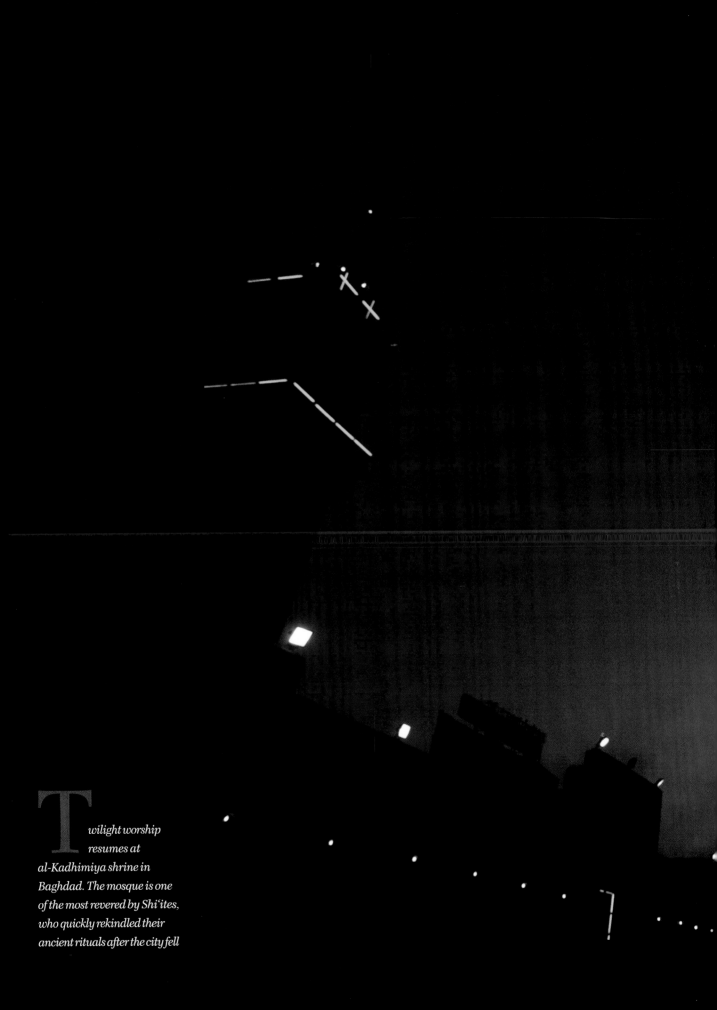

T wilight worship
resumes at
al-Kadhimiya shrine in
Baghdad. The mosque is one
of the most revered by Shi'ites,
who quickly rekindled their
ancient rituals after the city fell

CONQUEST AND CHAOS

HOW AMERICA BEAT SADDAM'S ARMY BUT WAS
BESIEGED BY EVERYONE ELSE: LOOTERS, POWER
SEEKERS AND CITIZENS DEMANDING SECURITY
By Michael Elliott

After the War, a Moment of Whimsy

A Marine indulges in an age-old impulse at Saddam Hussein's palace in his hometown of Tikrit. The Marines had expected furious resistance from regime loyalists in this city, but it never materialized

Photograph by Ashley Gilbertson—Aurora

We all know how we like wars to end. Ticker-tape parades, a sailor stealing a kiss on V-J day in Times Square, the French cheering the American

troops that entered Paris in 1944—those are the sort of images that we would choose, if we could, to bring every war to its close. But just below the surface, we know that even for the winners, wars aren't only like that; we've flicked through too many family photo albums with pictures of dads and brothers and cousins who didn't come home. We've seen cities reduced to heaps of stinking rubble, had our heartstrings tugged by the sight of maimed and orphaned children. There's a reason people look joyful when wars end; their smiles signal relief that a horror has abated.

Trying to Create Order from Anarchy

A member of the newly recruited, American-trained Free Iraq Forces shapes up in Nasiriyah. The force was bound for Baghdad, where it would work with U.S. troops to try to impose stability on a city gone out of control

In that respect, the war in Iraq was like all wars before it. This war's iconic moment of joy and relief came on April 9, when a U.S. team tied a chain to a statue of Saddam in Baghdad's Paradise Square and, with a couple of hefty yanks, pulled it from its pedestal. The monument was a tawdry example of Saddamite realism that would not have been out of place in Stalin's Soviet Union; within minutes, Iraqis were beating the statue with their shoes in the local expression of contempt. As U.S. soldiers spread out around Baghdad, driving down streets lined with date palms and mulberry trees, smiling people welcomed them, cheering and waving, offering cookies and water. "Thank you, Mr. Bush!" they cried. "We very like Mr. Bush!"

But even in the hours of liberation, war's scarred and ugly face showed itself. After years of brutal repression, there were scores to settle in Iraq, and settled they were. As they began to believe that Saddam's hated regime really was a thing of the past, Iraqis, from Basra in the south to Kirkuk in the north, started to turn on the Baath Party officials at whose whim people had been dragged off to torture chambers.

Though sporadic violence continued long after

Saddam's regime fell, the coalition forces had won a decisive victory. That was hardly surprising. The American military, with its astonishing technological prowess, was always going to roll over an Iraqi military that had been weakened by Gulf War I and years of sanctions. But three factors, in particular, seem to have been crucial.

The first—and still the least understood—was the role of special forces, especially in the northern theater of operations. In March, after much

New Uses for a Regime's Excesses

Outside of Saddam's Faruq Palace in Tikrit, a U.S. Marine walks a sentry beat past a laundry line rigged by his buddies. Below, freed prisoners of Baghdad's Al Hakemiya detention center survey part of their former quarters, where they were interrogated by secret police

Saddam Heads for The Souvenir Bin

To the bemusement of passersby, a man carts off the head of the Iraqi leader's statue that had been toppled before TV cameras in Baghdad's Paradise Square and then dragged through the streets by citizens

Photograph by James Nachtwey—VII

It's up to the Americans what this becomes. Maybe it will be colonialism, maybe it will be liberation from the regime. The truth will soon become apparent."

NAZIR MUSTAFA, Baghdad resident, watching U.S. tanks roll down the street

contention and confusion, the Turkish parliament decided it would not allow the 4th Infantry Division of the U.S. Army to invade Iraq from southeastern Turkey. This meant that much of the fighting in the north had to be done by Kurdish fighters backed by U.S. special forces and—after parachuting in on March 26—by members of the 173rd Airborne Brigade of the U.S. Army. But special forces ranged well beyond the north. After the success of the 2001 Afghanistan campaign, U.S. Defense Secretary Donald Rumsfeld was determined that the speed and flexibility of special forces gave the coalition an edge. From the earliest days of the war—and perhaps before—American, British and Australian commandos were at work, especially in the western desert, where they quickly seized two important airfields. They also attempted to secure the porous border with Syria and cut off an escape route for Iraqi officials who, the Administration alleged, were trying to find safe haven for themselves and whatever cash and valuables they could loot.

Just as crucial to success was the performance of the British forces in the south. The 7th Armored Brigade British Desert Rats were assigned the task of taking and holding Basra, the main city in that region, and the British Royal Marines were to take Iraq's only port, at Umm Qasr. This was gradually accomplished by a mixture of old-fashioned siege and lightning surgical strikes on targets of opportunity. It allowed U.S. Army and Marine units to sweep north on a march to the capital that was faster, it was later claimed, than any such advance in history—and to do so without having to worry about a breakout by elements of the Iraqi army to their rear. In the process, Iraq's massive southern oil fields were captured without sustaining major damage.

For Barbie, It's Liberation Day
To his son's amazement, this man carried off a door painted with a likeness of a doll from the villa of Saddam's stepbrother Watban Ibrahim Hassan. Property tied to the regime was among the first to be looted, but almost everything became fair game
Photograph by Yuri Kozyrev

No Longer Banking On Saddam in Kirkuk

Baghdad was not the only city in flames. When the Kurds reclaimed Kirkuk, they were unable to prevent looting of government properties. Here, a bank burns while a man and a child carry away some foam rubber they retrieved

Photograph by Yunghi Kim—Contact

Clearing War's Gruesome Detritus

Soldiers from the 3rd Infantry drag the body of a civilian into a trench after he was killed in the cross fire of a skirmish in a Baghdad suburb. About 10 combatants and civilians died, and their bodies were temporarily buried in a defensive trench that had been dug by the Iraqi army

But perhaps more important than anything was the sheer weight of coalition firepower, both from the air and on the ground. In the early days of the war, when fedayeen irregulars had caused all kinds of trouble for the invading armies in southern Iraq, it was assumed that Saddam's Republican Guard and Special Republican Guard—deployed in arcs in and around Baghdad — would fight with heroic intensity. That didn't happen. Outside the city the Republican Guard, for the most part, survived the aerial bombardment of its positions by coalition forces. (U.S. firepower was astonishingly accurate; in the market of the town of Mahmudiyah, five tanks parked in alleyways were hit while surrounding buildings were left intact.) But as U.S. ground troops approached, the Guard members fled, trading their army boots for less conspicuous sandals, throwing their weapons away, slinking back to their homes.

For some Iraqi officers, the memory of the capitulation was a bitter one. "We never fought," said a colonel who survived. "I am ashamed of what happened." In the wider Arab world, where the first few difficult days of the war had led to hopes that the U.S. would get at least a bloody nose before it deposed Saddam, the sudden collapse of Iraqi forces was humiliating. "To see our dignity wiped out like that, I am ashamed to be an Arab," said a Cairo physician. In Washington, by contrast, the speed of the victory led, predictably enough, to a degree of gloating. "The conclusion of the war will mark one of the most extraordinary military campaigns ever conducted," said Vice President Dick Cheney.

The campaign was indeed extraordinary, and

given the second guessing of the Administration's strategy by the brigade of retired generals in the TV studios, Cheney's satisfaction was understandable. Still, the war did not end neatly with the fall of Baghdad. As coalition forces mopped up in the city and moved north to Saddam's hometown of Tikrit, they continued to face fire from irregular forces and the remnants of the Iraqi army. In the three weeks after the statue in Paradise Square was toppled, 24 U.S. soldiers lost their lives. The number of Iraqis who died in the same period—because of coalition fire, vengeance killings or accidents like the explosion of ammunition dumps—may never be known. Plainly, however, the success of the coalition forces did not immediately make Iraq a safe and harmonious place.

First came the looting. From time immemori-

al, the chaos that goes with the end of a war has acted as an invitation—offered equally to soldiers and civilians alike—to make off with as much plunder as they could carry. The war in Iraq was an exception only insofar as American troops, by virtue of a killjoy order from the brass, were strictly enjoined from taking souvenirs back home. (One group of U.S. soldiers did succumb to temptation, however, and squirreled away $12.3 million in fresh $100 bills before they were apprehended.) But Iraqis were subject to no restraints. Some of them, surely, looted because they hated Saddam and all his works. Trashing the offices of his regime was a way of giving their hate concrete form. But other Iraqis, certainly, looted with criminal intent, grabbing goods that could be sold on the black market.

A Room with a View Of Destruction

A 3rd Infantry soldier conducts surveillance from what was once the lap of luxury. He's sitting among the ruins of the swimming pool that was situated on the third floor of Saddam's presidential palace in downtown Baghdad

Photographs by Christopher Morris—VII

**Through the Haze
Of a Lost Regime**
Marines guard an approach
to Tikrit at the edge of town.
The city fell largely without
a fight, its defenders
vanishing as the Marines
approached. The capture of
Saddam's hometown
marked the end of war,
although not of danger

Photograph by
Thomas Dworzak—Magnum

Religious Tradition Returns to Karbala

The end of the 40-day mourning period honoring the death of the Shi'ite martyr Imam Hussein is marked by pilgrims who crawl on their hands and knees to the Abu Fadel Al-Abbas shrine. Such rituals had been banned by Saddam

Photograph by
Yuri Kozeyrev

The devastation of the Iraq Museum on April 11 was probably a bit of both. Some of it was done by ordinary folk who saw a chance to get an artifact that could be sold for food; some of it, undoubtedly, was the work of professionals who knew exactly what they were looking for. Within days of the tragedy, an art smuggler called a dealer in Iraqi antiques, saying he had Japanese clients interested in anything that had come out of Iraq. It is true that, within a month, some of the artifacts that were thought to have gone missing had been returned, and others were discovered in safe keeping. But the trashing of the museum—and of the National Library and National Archives, together with important museums and collections in Basra and Mosul—represented an incalculable loss of treasures tracing a line back to the birth of civilization.

The truly curious thing about the looting was this: coalition forces seemed unprepared for it.

Although the U.S. had moved swiftly to secure the Oil Ministry building in Baghdad, little had been done to protect the Iraq Museum—despite the fact that American scholars had alerted the Pentagon to the need to secure its treasures. Similarly, U.S. officials seemed surprised by some of the first political developments in Iraq after the war ended. The Pentagon quickly landed Ahmed Chalabi, the leader of the exiled Iraqi National Congress, together with 600 fighters of his newly formed Free Iraqi Forces. But in the early days of the occupation, Chalabi, who promptly took up residence in a well-heeled suburb of Baghdad, seemed to engender little indigenous support. The best organized groups in Iraq, it appeared, were those of Shi'ite Muslims, who had been persecuted by Saddam's regime. Very quickly, Shi'ites, led by their imams, organized basic services in their own neighborhoods. In April hundreds of thou-

> "Whether you're Sunni or Shi'a or Kurd or Chaldean or Assyrian or Turkoman or Christian or Jew or Muslim, no matter what your faith, freedom is God's gift to every person in every nation."
>
> **PRESIDENT GEORGE W. BUSH**, in an address to jubilant Iraqi Americans in Dearborn, Mich.

As Guns Fall Silent, Mourning Begins

At the sprawling Shi'ite cemetery in Najaf, a woman grieves at the family plot and grave site of a relative who was killed by U.S. soldiers during the takeover of Baghdad, according to his family

Photograph by
James Nachtwey—VII

sands of them—flagellating themselves, beating their breasts with a noise of rolling thunder—made the pilgrimage to the shrine of Ali, the son-in-law of the Prophet Muhammad, in Karbala. Whoever ruled Iraq, it was clear, would have to take account of a resurgence of Shi'ite power.

It was not that the coalition forces were unwelcome. In the Kurdish north, in particular, Jay Garner, the retired U.S. Army Lieut. General who was initially placed in charge of reconstruction, was greeted as a hero and friend. But as civilian administrators gradually came into Iraq to begin the thankless but vital work of restoring basic services like electricity and clean water, the immensity of their challenge became plain. (Garner's recipe for success was succinct. "We ought to look in the mirror, stick out our chests, suck in our bellies and say, 'Damn, we're Americans,' and smile," he said.) Within a few weeks, it was

announced that Garner would be replaced—ahead of schedule—by a civilian, former ambassador Paul Bremer. Whoever was in charge, the key challenges remained the same. Should important jobs go to bureaucrats of the old regime—even if they had been members of the Baath Party? How much power should Shi'ite imams get? What sort of forum would be best suited to try to find representative Iraqi political leaders, and how quickly should it be convened? And this catalog didn't even touch on two matters of business that the war's end had not sorted out. Where were Saddam and his sons? Where were the weapons of mass destruction whose supposed existence had been the principal justification for the war in the first place?

In Washington, those who had planned and won the war had all these questions on their plate—and more. The success of the military cam-

Taking a Dip Into Liberation

A youth dives into a swimming pond once owned by Saddam Hussein. It is at the Kasser al-Tahadi palace in Mosul, Iraq's northern oil center, a Kurdish city before the regime drove the Kurds out. They are reclaiming it

Photograph by
Yunghi Kim—Contact

Here's Not Looking at You

The cult of Saddam was unavoidable in Iraq, his face as ubiquitous as windows. To coalition forces and Iraqis, each icon taken was a chance for symbolic victory by disfigurement. Here, the honor went to the Marines in Tikrit

Photograph by James Hill—Getty

paign in Iraq, Secretary of State Colin Powell said, had ushered a "new environment" into the Middle East. Powell and other members of the Administration lost no time in warning Syria, which was accused of sheltering Baath Party cronies, that it had to mend its ways and disavow terrorism. With less of a drum roll, the same message was sent to Tehran. And the Bush Administration took advantage of the end of Saddam's rule—plus the appointment of a new Prime Minister in Palestine—to unveil its long-awaited road map for peace between Israelis and Palestinians. All sides recognized, however, that precisely how and in what fashion the war in Iraq would really change the larger politics of the Middle East were questions that would not be answered for months—or years.

In Iraq itself, to say nothing of the hundreds of towns and cities where the loved ones of coalition forces awaited their heroes' return, high international politics was less important than relief over a hated dictator's removal from power and joy that a relative was coming home safely. But the duality that goes with the end of war continued, as it always does. Untold thousands of Iraqis had been killed, and by mid-May, 186 members of coalition forces were lost. Their families prepared not to meet their dad or mom, son or daughter, but to put a picture of their dead hero in pride of place. And Samira Jabar, a farmer's wife from outside Karbala, remembered her 6-year-old daughter Duaa, who, on April 6, had bent over to pick up a black plastic object attached to a white ribbon—a munition from a cluster bomb—that later exploded and ripped her body in half. "We thought we were safe because the bombs had stopped," said Jabar. Wars, sadly for her—and for us—rarely end the way we would like. ∎

Smooth Landing
For The Top Gun

President George W. Bush
greets a color-coded flight-
deck crew after landing on
the carrier U.S.S. *Abraham
Lincoln* as the ship returned
from action in the gulf. In a
speech on board, Bush
declared an end to the
combat phase of Gulf War II

**Photograph by
Brooks Kraft—Corbis**

CONTRIBUTORS

Simon Robinson Correspondent

James Nachtwey Photographer

Robert Nickelsberg Photographer

Christopher Morris Photographer

Our team of journalists covering the Iraq war included those who were embedded with troops and those who traveled independently. Either way, war reporting requires a special kind of journalist. Among those who contributed to this book:

SIMON ROBINSON
Our South Africa bureau chief traveled with the 1st Marine Division, riding into battle in the humvee of Lieut. Colonel Bryan McCoy, a fearless, lead-from-the-front officer. A Marine was shot and killed a few feet from Robinson at one point during a fire fight in Kut. "That was the first time it happened to someone in our battalion," he says. "There were bullets whizzing across the hood of our humvee. I was, frankly, very scared." Such stories, he says, never lack for drama. "You just have to survive to report them."

JIM LACEY
"Prolonged tedium punctuated with moments of high excitement" is how Lacey describes traveling with the vaunted 101st Airborne Division. There was plenty of action to make up for the downtime. Lacey witnessed 72 hours of fierce fighting during an assault on Najaf. Residents were initially suspicious of the invading troops, says Lacey, but "when they realized that the Americans were staying and that Saddam was gone, everything changed. The outpouring of support was incredible."

JAMES NACHTWEY
One of the world's most acclaimed photojournalists, he was recently featured, along with Christopher Morris, in the book *Shooting Under Fire*. Nachtwey debated whether to embed with U.S. troops before opting to work independently from Baghdad. There he recorded the sights of a city under attack—the damaged buildings, the bomb victims in hospital wards—and experienced the severe weather that hampered allied troops. "The sandstorm was the most amazing sight," says Nachtwey. "It looked like the prelude to an apocalypse."

BENJAMIN LOWY
Operation Iraqi Freedom was Lowy's first war. He learned fast, riding along with hundreds of military vehicles in a ground-assault convoy (GAC) of the 1st Brigade of the Army's 101st Airborne Division. Accompanying a squad of 15 soldiers, Lowy experienced the extremes of desert fighting: the stifling afternoons and the nights so cold that men sometimes used plastic bottles of their own urine as hand warmers. "When I got out of here," he says, "I wanted to make up a T shirt that said I SURVIVED THE GAC."

YURI KOZYREV
"It's in extreme situations," says Kozyrev, "that you get to see human nature and genuine emotions in all their intensity." As a man who has photographed conflicts in the republics of the former Soviet Union, Kozyrev, a Russian, should know. Situated in Baghdad, he found himself in another intense situation, as bombs pounded the city. "What has impressed me," he says, "is that the morale of the people remained high."

SALLY B. DONNELLY
While posted to Moscow in the mid-'90s, Donnelly also covered Russia's gory conflict, still going on, in the breakaway republic of Chechnya. Today she's the aviation correspondent for TIME. She usually works that beat from our Washington bureau, but when the war started, she was assigned the U.S. military's nerve center in Qatar. It was hundreds of miles from the battlefield, but for Donnelly, that safe distance was just fine this time. "This was as close as I wanted to get to the battlefield," she says, "now that I'm a wife and a mom of two."

ROBERT NICKELSBERG
Like most of our photographers, Nickelsberg relied on satellite telephone to transmit his pictures whenever his convoy—in the 3rd Battalion of the 1st Marine Division—came to an occasional halt. When the Marines secured the town of Tahrir, about 100 miles south of Baghdad, Nickelsberg followed as they went house to house, rounding up high-profile civilians for questioning. "They also entered the local police station," he says, "and removed the police."

JAMES HILL
Heading north on Iraqi Highway 1, Hill got an awful taste of the risks of embedding. His Marine convoy was ambushed by Iraqis dug into trenches along the side of the road who fired on the line of vehicles when they came within range. The Marines returned fire effectively, killing some of their attackers. "Whatever advantage technology offers," says Hill, "it's the spirit of those who fight that set the tone for this war."

CHRISTOPHER MORRIS
Over his 20-year career, Morris has seen plenty of combat, from Congo to Kosovo. This time, like many of the soldiers he accompanied, Morris left behind a family when he embarked for Kuwait. He and his wife have two daughters, the younger one born just a week before he departed.

Morris embedded with the Army's 3rd Infantry Division, the spearpoint of the drive north. The mixture of sandstorms and rain along the way sometimes left his cameras caked with a cement-like coating that he had to chip away bit by bit.

ALEX PERRY
"One of the most remarkable things about covering the war with the U.S. Army," says Perry, who was embedded with a combat unit of the 3rd Infantry Division, "is how close to home we were on the other side of the world." There were nightly showings of Hollywood movies on DVD and "enough peanut butter and jelly for, well, an army." What disturbed him, however, was just how little he and the troops knew of the people around them and the ancient land they inhabit. "I see others—Bedouins camping in the desert, families turning their cars around as they spot our approaching tanks—but they remain out of reach. I know I'll be back to explore whatever passes for peace in Iraq."

MICHAEL WARE
A veteran of conflicts in Indonesia, the South Pacific and Afghanistan, Ware spent Gulf War II in mountainous northern Iraq, where he tracked the shadowy strategies of U.S. special forces and anti-Saddam Kurdish fighters. Says Ware: "In the blood and mud and snow, you took it as you found it." But, he says, "it's the simplest things you remember most. I will always have the image before me of silent city workers with scarves over their faces collecting the bodies of the unclaimed dead of al-Qaeda-allied terrorists. And I will always remember the ecstatic Kurdish looters in an incandescent twilight waving a Britney Spears poster discarded in an Iraqi army bunker."